This book is a refreshing insight into the importance of each individual's responsibility to be a worshiper. God is looking for worshipers, and our privilege is to find our full potential. Patrick's insight and revelation make the book a tool that will assist worshipers everywhere.

David Hadden
Director, Academy of Worship, St. Louis, Missouri

Kavanaugh has put into words intuitions many of us have had since the Jesus Movement. But more than that, he articulates Christ-centered truths more wonderful than we have imagined. This is a liberating, creative, biblical book—not remotely a "how-to," but rather a "why" and, most significantly, a "Who." I have been waiting for this book a long time.

Michael Card, recording artist

I can't think of a more timely book for the Church today. Well-written, powerfully relevant and deeply inspiring. I guarantee this book will lead you into deeper intimacy with our awesome God.

Rory Noland
Music Director, Willow Creek Community Church
Author, *The Heart of the Artist*

Patrick Kavanaugh has written a helpful book looking at worship from a number of different perspectives. In particular I recommend his desire to learn from different traditions within the Christian community and to formulate an understanding based on the best that each of these traditions has to offer. The book will provide a useful introduction to the subject for young Christians, while encouraging more mature Christians to grow in their devotional lives. Some aspects of the subject may be unfamiliar to some sections of the worshiping community, and this book could be helpful in raising discussion on a range of issues.

Christopher Redgate
Lecturer in music and worship, London Bible College, England

worship—
a way of life

Other Books by Patrick Kavanaugh

Spiritual Lives of the Great Composers (Zondervan)
Raising Musical Kids (Vine)
Music of the Great Composers (Zondervan)
The Music of Angels: A Listener's Guide to Sacred Music from Chant to Christian Rock (Loyola)
Spiritual Moments with the Great Composers (Zondervan)

Books by Patrick and Barbara Kavanaugh

Devotions from the World of Music (Cook)

worship—
a way of life

Patrick Kavanaugh

Chosen Books
A Division of Baker Book House Co
Grand Rapids, Michigan 49516

Published by Chosen Books
a division of Baker Book House Company
P.O. Box 6287, Grand Rapids, MI 49516-6287

Second printing, February 2002

Printed in the United States of America

Library of Congress Cataloging-in-Publication Data

Kavanaugh, Patrick.
    Worship—a way of life / Patrick Kavanaugh.
        p.   cm.
    ISBN 0-8007-9292-0 (pbk.)
    1. Worship. I. Title.
BV10.2 .K38 2001
248.3—dc21   2001028563

Scripture is taken from the HOLY BIBLE, NEW INTERNATIONAL VERSION®. NIV®. Copyright © 1973, 1978, 1984 by International Bible Society. Used by permission of Zondervan Publishing House. All rights reserved.

For current information about all releases from Baker Book House, visit our web site:

http://www.bakerbooks.com

This book is gratefully dedicated to
my dear friends John and Roslyn Langlois,
who have been a steadfast example
for all of us who worship the Lord.

"Seven whole days, not one in seven I will praise Thee;
Even eternity's too short to extol Thee."

George Herbert (1593–1633)

Contents

Foreword

The advance of renewal throughout the Church has been progressing at "Lightspeed" over the entire past century. That is to say, wherever people *open* to the *"Light"* of God's Word, there are increasing evidences of God's *"speed"* in advancing His Kingdom as He manifests His readiness to *fulfill* His Word.

As a student of recent Church history, a teacher of God's Word and a pastor to Christ's flock for more than four decades, I've had opportunity to observe and confirm what more and more are noting as obvious: Where *worship* is awakened or renewed, the *vital life* of the Holy Spirit flows, blows, glows and ignites something among those worshipers.

The worship of God, along with the subject of praying to Him, has themed more books over the centuries than any other among His people. From schedules for liturgical observance to descriptions of raw revival where spiritual breakthrough confronts human tastes and humbles human pride, people write about worship, its exercise and the expectations attending it. As I said in the introduction to one of my own books on this theme, "So why another book?" Let me answer that as I invite you to pursue the one you have in hand.

- "Another book" because the Holy Spirit keeps doing new and refreshing things, and it is arrogance not to expect that creative newness may find expression *anywhere*, seeing the One we worship is a tireless Creator!
- "Another book" because there are always people who are unaware of the existence of all the others; because there are circles of influence opened to some writers and leaders that are brand new fields of service with all new things to be discovered by those in that arena.
- "Another book" because God loves to *uniquely* incarnate facets and features of His will, way, wisdom—*His Word!*— in *uniquely* distinct and beautiful ways through His *uniquely* fashioned giftings in each of His *uniquely* loved sons and daughters. In short: *It is inevitable that there is something about worship here that you've never come across before!*

Patrick Kavanaugh is an established voice in calling us all to worship, but better than that, he's a *passionate* voice! As you read you will discover he is not asking you to *analyze* worship, but to be open to *catalyze* it! And that's why the worship renewal sweeping across the earth continues—because the subject is moving from the inside out; instead of trying to *get* things going "at Church," to being willing to *let* things happen in your own soul.

Worship that becomes a lifestyle at a personal level will be certain to change the worship life of any church at a congregational level. Whether you're a leader, asking the Holy Spirit to help you find keys to renewal as you seek to lead others in worship, or you're a church member, hungering and thirsting for freshness and new, Holy Spirit-stimulated vitality in the church family you love and attend, here's something for you.

Here's a sensible, spiritually insightful look at worship, with a lot to help us all at multiple dimensions. So go ahead. Take another step forward in your own personal renewal, and stride at even a brisker pace with the throng marching forward in worship around the world. And when you're done with this book, I think I know what you'll probably say.

"That *wasn't 'just another book!'*"

Jack W. Hayford, Pastor/Chancellor
The Church On The Way
The King's College and Seminary

Acknowledgments

A book of this scope is never created without the help of many talented people, more than I could possibly hope to thank, but I cannot forgo mentioning the following:

The other directors of the Christian Performing Artists' Fellowship—the Krafts, the Langlois, the Lamberts, the Sturms and the Tavanis—for their continued support and encouragement of this work.

Jane Campbell, Ann Weinheimer and the staff of Chosen Books, for superb editing and ongoing committment to excellence.

To the most resourceful of research assistants, Janice Norris, for working through dozens of enigmatic problems and finding many obscure facts that are now in this book.

For my four wonderful sons—Chris, John, Peter and David—for their understanding and love, even when Dad had to finish typing his book when he would rather have been playing with them.

Acknowledgments

For my best friend and dear wife, Barbara, for her unflagging support and invaluable companionship—not to mention tireless proofreading.

For three men who have been spiritual mentors in my life: Derrel Emmerson, David Shropshire and Bill Jeschke. Keep worshiping!

Introduction

The purpose of this book is to bring the reader closer to Christ. Specifically, it is written to help each of us worship the Lord—to worship Him with deeper intimacy, with purer love, with greater potency. It is something every Christian can do more every day. Whether you are a new believer or an experienced pastor—or anyone in between these extremes in the Christian walk—all of us need to worship God more with each year of our lives.

There are many excellent books available today concerning how to improve our relationships with one another, how to be servants to each other, how to better our marriages, our child-rearing, etc. These are all tremendously important subjects, more so today than ever. But this book is not about any of these topics. It is simply about God and you. It is about worship.

Of course, the topic of Christian worship in the last two thousand years is ponderous enough to fill many volumes. Indeed, just to cover all the various styles of worship today would be too ambitious for one book. Rather than attempt a comprehensive study, I have elected to focus on the personal side of worship. Rather than concentrate on the outward manifestations—the "things people do" when they are worshiping—I will contemplate what is happening on a deeper level: the intimate relationship that each of us can and should have with our Lord.

Certain worship styles in churches today, and to which I will refer, are somewhat controversial and uncomfortable for many of us. But this book is not to judge. I do not have a hidden agenda either to condemn or condone any particular worship style. Rather, I believe that all Christians can learn from each other in the area of worshiping God.

Imagine a large bonfire on a cold night. There are a dozen or so other people with you, and together you make a large and complete circle around the fire. Let us further imagine that all of you are Christians but from completely different church backgrounds, with most of the major denominations and theological viewpoints represented. The bonfire symbolizes God Himself.

Using this illustration, I would say that the purpose of this book is to encourage all of us to draw closer to the warmth of the fire. It matters little whether you are a Presbyterian or a Baptist. It matters even less if you are a Scripture scholar or a child. Each person in the circle becomes warmer, not by looking at each other or trying to appraise one another but by coming closer to the source of heat.

It is not a matter of "where you are coming from." It is very much a matter of "what direction you are *moving toward*."

My ministry brings me into contact with hundreds of Christians from a wide variety of denominational and non-denominational heritages. As Executive Director of the Christian Performing Artists' Fellowship (CPAF) and Artistic Director of the MasterWorks Festival, I work with believers who come from backgrounds including Bible Church, Baptist, Presbyterian, Lutheran, Episcopal, Anglican, Assembly of God, AME, Catholic Church of Christ, Methodist . . . you name it!

Concerning some of the more controversial topics of the day, I work with Christians who are strongly charismatic (who prophesy, speak in tongues, etc.), Christians who believe that charismatics are all deceived, Christians who spend hours "laughing in the Spirit," and Christians who believe that anyone who "laughs in the Spirit" is insane.

It is an interesting job that I have.

In addition to working with CPAF, I have also been a minister of music for more than twenty years. I have had the privilege of helping churches worship God with a unity that cannot be explained in human terms. I have taken part in hundreds of worship services that seem to break through the clouds and approach the Throne Room of the Almighty. And I have known the beauty and intimacy of privately sitting before the Lord Jesus and truly worshiping Him "in Spirit and in Truth."

Yet, as I wrote in my last book, *The Music of Angels: A Listener's Guide to Sacred Music from Chant to Christian Rock*, I have also had the opposite experience. I have had the misfortune to see music and worship—or rather, the mishandling of music and worship—create terrible schisms in the Christian Church. It sometimes seems that there are more "church splits" over style of worship than over biblical doctrine.

There is a tremendous need for believers to break down the walls that have separated us. We can learn so much from one another on the subject of worship. This will bring us not only closer to each other as Christians but closer to Christ. Rather than further divide the Body of Christ, we can come together in our worship of the Living God.

So I pray that this book will play a part in bringing believers into closer communion with our Lord. If it does this for even one reader, it will have been well worth the effort.

part 1

Why Worship?

chapter one

What Is Worship?

"But the LORD, who brought you up out of Egypt with mighty power and outstretched arm, is the one you must worship. To him you shall bow down and to him offer sacrifices."

2 Kings 17:36

Worship is the submission of all of our nature to God. It is the quickening of conscience by his holiness, nourishment of mind by his truth, purifying of imagination by his beauty, opening of the heart to his love, and submission of will to his purpose. All this gathered up in adoration is the greatest of all expressions of which we are capable.

William Temple, Archbishop of Canterbury

Has "Harold" Been to *Your* Church?

Let us suppose that an angel has been sent to earth.

He is a young angel, still in angel high school, and has a difficult homework assignment. It is his task to write a term paper on "Worship Within Christianity." He has a lot of research to do. He is, of course, experienced in all forms of angelic worship styles, but he has never been to earth and has no idea how humans worship the Lord Jesus Christ.

Now he is determined to find out. In order not to alarm the humans he will meet, it was decided that he be invisible as he observes their times of worshiping God.

We will call our young angel "Harold."

To help Harold write his term paper, his teacher gave him an outline. Unrolling his golden scroll, Harold looked at his outline for the first topic. He saw the question "1. What Is Worship?"

This is an easy one, thought Harold. *I already know what worship is. I simply have to see how the earthlings would answer such a question. Perhaps I'll visit a few churches and finish this quickly.*

Unfortunately, it did not work out quite as he had expected. After visiting three different churches in the same town—all of which would have answered the question "What Is Worship?" very differently—Harold decided to continue his visits throughout the earth. He encountered more variety. With every visit he found the same confusing results.

Among many others, Harold witnessed the following expressions of worship:

- in a large beautiful church in Dallas, Texas, a man said to the congregation, "Let us now worship," and they sang three slow hymns;
- in a small storefront church in Washington, D.C., the congregation sang loudly for two hours, the music punctuated by screams, prophecies and people falling to the floor;

24

- in an outdoor meeting near Nairobi, Kenya, the people worshiped by singing highly rhythmic songs accompanied by intricate clapping and the use of many percussion instruments;
- in a very old church in Moscow, Russia, the congregation stood silently throughout the long service, but many of them often bowed deeply to the floor;
- in a student service at the University of Illinois in Chicago, the young people (those not playing guitars) raised their hands while singing and often "spoke in tongues" and "sang in the Spirit";
- in a Church of Christ service in Nashville, Tennessee, no instruments were heard; the congregation sang a number of lovely unaccompanied hymns;
- in a mass in Venice, Italy, the congregation listened to the words of the priest, often reciting words themselves and changing positions: kneeling, sitting, standing;
- in a large auditorium in Toronto, Ontario, the congregation not only "sang in the Spirit," but also spent an extended time "laughing in the Spirit";
- in a drive-in theater in San Diego, California, the congregation was led by a large rock band with volume loud enough to be heard in the next county;
- in an "on-line" church meeting, dozens of participants from all parts of the globe keyed in their favorite songs in an act of worship from their computer terminals at home.

Harold was rather confused by these episodes, as they were quite different from the customary worship of the angels around the throne of God. Yet in each of his many experiences, Harold sensed Christians present who were truly worshiping the Lord Jesus Christ with all their hearts.

He wondered at the many differences he encountered. Would the people in the Dallas church be able to worship God at the storefront church in Washington, D.C.? Or the other way around? Would the young people from the Chicago university find the same joy in worshiping at the Venice mass? What about the congregations from Moscow or Nairobi—could they be taught to "worship God online"?

Harold was not too sure about all this.

Like high school students all around the universe, he realized that this project might take more time than he had originally thought. Harold quickly went back to his school and sought his teacher to request a special dispensation: that he might revisit some of the churches and assume a human form at will. Permission granted, Harold was now able to blend in with the crowd and actually speak to members of the congregations.

Harold Meets the Christians

Harold spoke to an older couple leaving the Dallas church the next Sunday. After a few polite comments about the sermon, he asked them, "What do you like about the worship here at your church?"

The woman said, "They have a great choir, and they always sing my favorite hymns."

Her husband answered, "The minister of music is a great guy, and he picks hymns that really convey the Gospel message."

Later that day, Harold talked with several young people leaving the San Diego rock service. When he asked them, "What do you like about the worship here?" everyone wanted to talk at once.

"The worship here is awesome!" exclaimed one girl. "It makes me feel so close to God."

Another said, "I just close my eyes during the worship and I can imagine Jesus wrapping His arms around me. It's fantastic!"

Harold spoke with many people around the world as they exited their churches. The same question elicited a wide variety of answers, but most were very positive. The humans seem to like the way their own churches worshiped, and each seemed to assume that *this* was the way Christians worship God.

Sometimes in these conversations, Harold would mention various other expressions of worship that he had witnessed around the world. Usually those around him would stare in amazement and occasionally in disgust.

One man declared, "No true Christian would worship God by shouting and falling on the floor."

Another said, "Stand there and not say a word? That sounds like a cult to me."

Still another remarked, "Only dead churches still sing those worn-out old hymns."

Finally, one insisted, "No church should ever use that horrible rock music!"

Harold wondered greatly at such reactions, especially at the strong emotion. It seemed that humans loved to worship God in their individual ways, but did not accept others' worship of God unless it matched their own traditions.

He resolved to try a different approach.

Harold Researches Private Worship

Harold decided that his research had been concentrating too much on the humans' *corporate* worship experiences. Perhaps the many differences would be minimized in the humans' *private* worship. Once more he engaged people in conversations.

After talking awhile with an older gentleman leaving church, Harold asked, "Do you ever worship like this at home, during the week, alone with God?"

"What's that?" the man stammered. "What do you mean?"

"Well," Harold began, "do you sing at home each day as you sang today at your church? Or do you have other means of private worship during the week?"

The man looked blankly at Harold. He finally said, "I'm not much of a singer. And what I do all week is certainly none of your business."

Poor Harold received similar reactions from many different individuals. Happily, there were exceptions. Occasionally someone would answer, "Yes, I love to sing praise songs at home." Harold was encouraged to hear that several mentioned reading the Bible during the week or praying with the family. But he found very few who spent time every day simply worshiping the Lord on their own.

The young angel Harold took a long time in his research, traveling to many parts of earth. He had to rewrite his outline twice and his golden scroll was quite messy by the time he finished his term paper. It began as follows:

"Worship Within Christianity" *—by Harold, Angel, Second Class*

"This was my first visit to earth, and I am very grateful to my teacher for allowing me to assume a human form and speak with the people. I had no idea that so many different traditions and practices existed among the Christians on earth in the area of worship.

"There are millions of Christians on earth who love the Lord Jesus very much. Yet they do not worship God in the same way that we do. Indeed, though they worship Him in many different ways, each dislikes the way others worship God. As strange as this seems to us, they often disagree so violently that *worship* has become one of the most divisive aspects of Christianity on earth.

"Most of the humans I met like to worship God only if they are in large groups, preferably directed by an energetic leader. Few take time to worship when they are alone. This peculiar tendency may result from their confusion between worship and 'worship music.' In fact, many Christians seemed to equate worshiping the Lord simply with singing Christian songs. For most, the only time they are consciously worshiping is when they are singing songs about God. And when the song stops, the worship time is over.

"Furthermore, there are furious debates about these songs among Christians on earth. It is not so much that certain humans *like* certain songs. It is rather that each human completely *despises* certain songs—or, rather, certain *types* of songs. This also has created great divisions and extraordinary controversy. In particular, it seems that the older a human becomes, the more he dislikes the songs of the younger Christians—who, in turn, reject the older Christian's songs.

"Many of their churches have, in addition to a pastor, a hired person whose job seems to be keeping the Christians in their church from fighting too ferociously against each other about their music and worship. He has the baffling job of trying to select worship songs that everyone might like, but this is seldom possible. This person is usually called a 'minister of music,' but I think a better title might be 'referee' or 'sheriff.' ..."

The State of the Art of Worship

The previous pages are, of course, rather fanciful. I do not know any angel named Harold who had to write a term paper on "Worship Within Christianity."

But suppose someone completely objective—someone outside of any Christian experience and without knowledge of our various traditions—could observe our multitudinous ways of worshiping God. To be a qualified and impartial judge, this person would already have to know what worship is (through personal experience) but not be biased toward any one tradition or denomination.

What would his comments be?

I suggest that they might be similar to those written above on Harold's golden scroll.

Of course, there are many wonderful exceptions to Harold's somewhat bewildering comments. Perhaps you are one. Perhaps your church is one. Wherever you or your church may be on the topic of worshiping God, we all have much we can learn.

The Supreme Preeminence of Worship

Worship ought to be our number-one priority on earth. When Jesus was asked, "What is the greatest commandment?" He answered, "'Love the Lord your God with all your heart and with all your soul and with all your mind.' This is the first and greatest commandment" (Matthew 22:37–38). After giving this supreme command, Jesus continued: "And the second is like it. 'Love your neighbor as yourself'" (Matthew 22:39).

Jesus gave the commandments in order for a reason: It is because the first must be *first*. It is no good trying to keep the second commandment until we have kept the first. It would be like trying to perform the second in a series of instructions before completing the first task. It does not work. It is not meant to.

Getting us to act on this supreme commandment has been the endeavor of all the great preachers and teachers throughout the last two millennia. This was the urging of Augustine in his masterpiece, *City of God:* "Let us love Him as we ought to love Him. For this is the great reward, this is royalty and pleasure, this is enjoyment, and glory, and honor, this is light, this is the great happiness, which language or reasoning cannot set before us nor mind conceive."

"All right," you concede, "we should love God first. But how *do* we love God? How else can we show Him our love except through keeping His command to love others?"

Jesus indeed made it clear that one of the ways we can show Him our love is by loving others. "Whatever you did for one of the least of these brothers of mine, you did for me" (Matthew 25:40). His emphasis on keeping the first commandment does not mean we are to ignore the second.

Nevertheless, this cannot be the only way we can show our love for God. Any individual ought to be able to express love to the Lord even if he or she were the only human left on earth. But how?

Spending Time with God

Anyone who has ever raised children knows that kids spell the word *love*, T-I-M-E. That is, if you want to show love to your children, you need to spend *time* with them. This is what they want from us—not things or money or lectures, etc. They want our time. There is no better way to show them our love.

For that matter, any relationship needs time. Those of us who are married might remember when we first met our spouses-to-be. We wanted to spend *all* our time with them! And after the honeymoon is long since over, a marriage still needs an investment of time spent together if it is to continue and grow. All friendships take time as we get to know one another and do things together that will cement the relationships.

Time is the ultimate stewardship. Each of us is given only so much and we must take care to spend it carefully, for if it is wasted or stolen we cannot get it back. Even Napoleon had to admit: "There is one kind of robber the law does not strike at, though he steals what is most precious to men: Time." The time we have is indeed precious, and how we spend it demonstrates to the world what is most important to us.

In the same way, if we want to show our love for God, it will cost us some time: time to spend with the Lord, time to get to know Him, time to prepare our hearts for His service. It takes time. But it is the most worthwhile investment of our time we can ever make.

During Jesus' three-year public ministry on earth, notwithstanding the wonderful teachings our Lord gave the crowds, He spent His time primarily with His disciples. Jesus would tell them, "Come with me by yourselves to a quiet place and get some rest" (Mark 6:31). Some of this was spent with the entire group of disciples, but the gospels also refer to times spent alone with specific disciples. Certainly these were often used for instruction, but much of the time was doubtless spent in nurturing their deep relationships. It took time.

One is reminded of Jesus' poignant words when He found His closest disciples asleep in Gethsemane: "Could you men not keep watch with me for one hour?" (Matthew 26:40).

This spending time with God—focusing on Him and putting aside the cares of the world—gives us time to mature in our relationship with Him. It is called worship. It may happen in large or small groups, generally known as corporate worship, or it may happen in private. Yet even in the largest group, worship is still a private experience between each worshiper and God. The group simply happens to be together in the same room, outwardly doing the same things (generally).

The Principle at Work in Relationships

Why is spending time with God so important?

Suppose you toss a pebble into a still pond. You see the ripples moving away from the point of impact, the concentric circles growing larger and larger. What you may not see is that as the ripples grow in circumference, the actual height of each ripple begins to decrease. That is, the waves closest to the center are the highest and as they progress outward they become gradually lower.

This principle, known to every physics major, gives us a picture we can use to describe the relative importance of each of our relationships. Let me use myself as an example. Like everyone else, I have relationships with many people, some close and some superficial. They include those with my family, extended family, friends, coworkers, etc.

According to the supreme two commandments Jesus gave us, the most important relationship I can have is with God. After Him, my wife is next. Then come my four sons. After that I place my closest friends, fellow-worshipers at church and coworkers. Soon come the unbelievers with whom I have relationships and those I hope to bring to Christ. You get the idea. The center of the concentric rings is God. The first ring is my wife, the next rings are my sons and so on.

But this is more than simple prioritizing. For just as each rippling wave in the pond can never be higher (that is, larger, more powerful) than a wave that is closer to the center, so it is with our relationships. For instance, I can never be any greater as a father than I am as a husband. Likewise, in God's perfect plan, my relationship with my wife must never be stronger than my relationship to the Lord.

This principle works throughout all of my relationships. Of course, I want them all to be strong. Yet if each can only be as strong as the next inner ring, then I absolutely must make sure that my relationship with God—the center ring—is truly strong and growing.

"Worshipful" Activities?

Perhaps now you are concluding, "Yes, I see that my relationship with the Lord is very important. But what does this have to do with worship?"

Perhaps this question should be rephrased as, "But what does this have to do with 'what is usually *called*' worship?"

Let us look at what worship is, and what it is not. If you ask a number of fellow-believers about certain activities that might be included in the realm of worship, you would probably assemble a list similar to the one below:

- singing together in the congregation on Sunday morning
- praying alone
- reading the Bible
- listening quietly to a musical solo at church
- meditating on the Lord and His Word
- having a small Bible study or prayer group
- interceding with God on behalf of others

Perhaps other believers would add further items, which might not immediately occur to you:

- listening to a sermon
- giving a sermon
- singing along with a Christian radio station or CD
- talking to God and listening for His voice

- playing a musical instrument for the Lord
- using any artistic gift (writing, acting, etc.) for the Lord
- witnessing to an unbeliever

There are many Christians who would also add:

- speaking in tongues
- interpreting tongues
- prophesying
- being "slain in the Spirit"
- singing in the Spirit
- dancing before the Lord
- laughing in the Spirit

And there are many mature Christians who would point out that anything done "in a spirit of worship" could be considered worship to the Lord. The list could now contain almost anything:

- washing the dishes
- mowing the grass
- walking the dog

This seems to present a problem. If worship is (or can be) *everything*, then we have come no closer to finding what it really is and what it is not.

When, Exactly, Does Worship Take Place?

Once while talking about this subject I was asked by a Christian friend, "Can *anything* be worship?" My initial response—which was motivated by a desire to encourage—was, "Of course! Everything we do can be an act of worship to God!"

But I was quickly challenged by the fact that certain actions condemned in Scripture could never be associated with worshiping the Lord. No one who is stealing or cheating, for example, can profess to be doing this as an act of worship—no matter how "spiritual" he may claim to be at the time. There are many sinful activities that cannot be linked with the true worship of God.

We find, therefore, that there are three broad categories into which we can place all of our actions:

1. "holy" actions, generally associated with worship (singing Christian songs, praying)
2. "commonplace" actions, which may or may not be done in a spirit of worship (washing the dishes, mowing the grass)
3. "evil" actions, during which no worship of God can take place (stealing, cheating)

We can conclude from this that worship cannot take place in those actions of the third category, and that worship *may* take place in those of the second category—depending upon the spiritual state of the worshiper. But what about those in the first category? Does performing a worshipful activity automatically make it worship? Are we always worshiping God while we are singing at church (or at home) or praying?

Would that it were so! We need to be very honest about this. Unfortunately, we all know that we can find ourselves singing praise to God while our minds stray to the football game we will see later that day or the roast we have to get into the oven. We can be praying sincerely one moment and be pondering the stock market the next. Or have you ever suddenly realized while reading the Bible that, though your eyes have continued to scan the page, you have been thinking of something completely unrelated for the last minute?

This is not a new problem. We have all been there. Each of us can identify with the great poet John Donne, who conceded: "I throw myself down in my chamber, and I call in and invite God and his angels thither; and when they are there, I neglect God and his angels for the noise of a fly, for the rattling of a

35

coach, or the whining of a door." And Shakespeare spoke for all of us in these lines:

> My words fly up, my thoughts remain below:
> Words without thoughts never to heaven go.

The good news is that God understands. He does not condemn us for the way we are made. He made us and, even with our many faults, still loves and forgives us. It is good to remember the words of David: "As a father has compassion on his children, so the LORD has compassion on those who fear him; for he knows how we are formed, he remembers that we are dust" (Psalm 103:13–14).

I know Christians who feel tremendous guilt because they find themselves thinking about something mundane in the middle of worship times. Certainly we should try to keep our focus on the Lord at such times and improve on this year to year in our Christian walk. But Scripture shows clearly that God is not angry with us when we lapse in our concentration.

This does not, of course, excuse lapses in concentration that might lead us to sinful actions. It is one thing for a man to find himself contemplating his busy schedule during a worship song. It is quite another if he finds himself contemplating the curves of the ladies in front of him.

The point here is simply that no actions we can perform, even the most sanctimonious, will guarantee that we are truly worshiping God. It is not a matter of activities. It is a matter of the heart.

What Takes Place in True Worship?

Think of it this way. Suppose a person were paralyzed as well as deaf and dumb. This person could not sing or lift his hands or even pray aloud. He could perform none of the outward physical activities associated with worship. Could a person in this extreme situation still worship God? Yes, indeed he could. This is not to suggest that our actions have nothing to do with worship. It is important to see, however, that true worship is not dependent on external actions.

To understand this, we need to examine what happens *internally* during a time of true worship.

We have listed many external actions that can take place during worship. Others you know from your own experience, either at your church, in small groups or in private. But we have also pointed out two significant conclusions that cause us to reconsider the entire subject:

1. It is possible for Christians to worship God while doing ordinary tasks (washing the dishes).
2. It is possible for Christians *not* to worship God while doing activities strongly related to worship (singing at church, praying).

Let us start with the lowest common denominator. That is, what must always occur for anyone to worship the Lord? The answer is "a consciousness of God."

Step 1: God-Consciousness

To many mature Christians this may seem so obvious that it hardly bears mentioning. But we must remember that there are millions of people walking around our cities at this moment who are not at all conscious of God. This does not mean that they are horrible, evil people. As a matter of fact, it includes everyone, believers and unbelievers, you and me.

These people are thinking about a plethora of other matters. We all are. If we did not we could hardly survive in this world. We still need to cook dinner and read the mail and pay the bills. Let's face it. Most of us do these activities without giving much thought to God.

Again, the Lord does not condemn us for thoughts that are not specifically "God-related." In the story of the two sisters, Mary and Martha (see Luke 10:38–42), Jesus did not rebuke the busy Martha for *what* she was doing around the house. The correction had to do with the inappropriate time she chose to be busy, a time when she should have been sitting and listening to Jesus. Later that evening, the Lord doubtless enjoyed the meal Martha had made and thanked her for her work and hospitality.

Fortunately for us, even when we are not actually conscious of God, He is always conscious of us. The renowned Russian writer Leo Tolstoy pointed out: "God is he without whom one cannot live." How often do we find comfort in these words in the Scriptures: "He will never leave you nor forsake you" (Deuteronomy 31:6)?

On the other hand, if we spend all our time in ordinary tasks and never think about God at all we are living in great error. The Bible contains dozens of verses commanding us to "set [our] hearts on things above," as Paul says in Colossians 3:1. In the very next verse he takes us further, admonishing us to "set [our] minds on things above, not on earthly things." We all have read hundreds of verses exhorting us to pray, sing, preach, meditate and worship God.

And we have been exhorted by the great men and women of the ages. President Calvin Coolidge once remarked: "It is only when men begin to worship that they begin to grow." And Thomas Carlyle insisted: "The man who does not habitually worship is but a pair of spectacles behind which there is no eye."

All worship must begin with a consciousness of God.

How does this sudden consciousness of God begin? Well, how does a conversation between any two people begin? Usually in one of two ways: one person starts the conversation or else the other person does. In the same way, our consciousness of God can be initiated by us or by the Lord Himself.

When we decide to pray or to sing praises or to read the Bible thoughtfully or to focus our thoughts on the Lord, *we* are initiating "God-consciousness." Indeed, this is exactly what the Bible continually tells us to do.

And by the same token, there are also countless times when God Himself initiates this. How many times have you been intent on some task before you when, suddenly, a Bible verse comes "out of nowhere"? Or you remember someone you should pray for? Or you abruptly look up and notice the beauty of God's earth and thank Him and praise Him for it? Indeed, Jesus told His disciples that the Holy Spirit would remind them of everything He had said to them (see John 14:26).

God does not limit His reaching out to believers only; He initiates a consciousness of Himself with unbelievers as well. Thousands of former atheists have testified how thoughts of God, unasked for and often resisted, filled their hearts unawares. Their experiences may not be as dramatic as Paul's on the Damascus road, but they are equally divine and authoritative. In all these cases, God is the initiator and we choose how we will respond.

Incidentally, there is also a third way in which God-consciousness can be initiated. Just as a conversation between two people can begin with either of them, there is also the possibility that they were brought together by a third party. That is, they could have been introduced to each other by an outside person or force.

This is exactly what happens to us on many Sunday mornings. We begrudgingly fall out of bed, stumble through our morning routines and drive to church. When we arrive, often bleary-eyed and exhausted, we are about as God-conscious as our shoes. Yet when we hear the strains of praise music in the sanctuary our heart begins to rise, and this "outside force" brings our thoughts back to the Lord. This third party of music (among other arts) illustrates one of the primary purposes of corporate worship and will be dealt with further in later chapters.

Step 2: Our Right Response to God

But is simply being in a state of "God-consciousness" enough? Is that all we are to attempt? Of course not. It is only the first step—an essential one to be sure, and no further steps can be made without the first one. But God-consciousness by itself is not worship.

In fact, the letter of James points out that, "You believe that there is one God. Good! Even demons believe that—and shudder" (James 2:19). In other words, anyone can be aware of God, but that is not worship. It is our *response* to God—whether we turn away from Him and run, or turn toward Him and worship—that is the critical issue.

In C. S. Lewis's marvelous series of books The Chronicles of Narnia, there are times when a number of different people first hear the name of Aslan (the Christ-figure in the story). Even before it is explained who Aslan is, their reactions are quite different: Some are strangely exhilarated and inspired; others are repelled and suspicious. Whether they become noble characters in the story or evil ones depends upon their response to Aslan.

A biblical parallel is given in 2 Corinthians 2:14–16, where Paul explains that God "through us spreads everywhere the fragrance of the knowledge of him. For we are to God the aroma of Christ among those who are being saved and those who are perishing. To the one we are the smell of death; to the other, the fragrance of life."

The fragrance is the same in both cases. It comes from the one God. But different people react in opposite ways: "To the one we are the smell of death; to the other, the fragrance of life."

As soon as we become God-conscious, at any given time of the day or night, we have choices to make. We can ignore it and get busy and distracted, or we can take the second step: We can make a right response to God.

If we take this second step, we put ourselves in right relationship with our Creator. This may result in outward manifestations: We may reach for a musical instrument and play a praise song; we may read aloud from His Word or get to work at what He may prompt us to do. Or it may result in inner manifestations: We may offer a prayer in the quietness of our hearts or remember a favorite Scripture; or we may enjoy a moment of inner bliss as we simply want to "be still, and know that I am God" (Psalm 46:10). Either way, it is worship.

Worship—the Growth of Our Relationship with God

Worshiping God is not a matter of singing or praying or doing. It is what happens when we become God-conscious (whether this is initiated by God or by ourselves) and we make a right response.

Does this sound too simple? For the angels, it probably is simple. Just ask "Harold."

But for most of us, there are a number of barriers that all too often keep both the first and the second steps from happening. These can come from the busy world around us, from our sinful natures, which prompt us to be self-centered, and from the enemy—who will attempt any trick possible to keep us from worshiping the Lord.

Nevertheless, it is possible to increase our sensitivity to God and to live our lives more and more in a state of worshiping God. The great saints of Christ have proven this many times throughout the ages. One thinks of Brother Lawrence's book of maxims, *The Practice of the Presence of God,* which illustrates his attitude of worship during the many years he worked in a monastery kitchen.

This practice of personal worship has been called by many names. It is what Oswald Chambers, in his devotional, *My Utmost for His Highest,* calls "Communion with God." Hannah Whitall Smith, in her classic work, *The Christian's Secret of a Happy Life,* speaks of the "unfathomable sweetness of consecration to God." In his book *The Pursuit of God,* A. W. Tozer calls it "the continuous and unembarrassed interchange of love and thought between God and the soul of redeemed man."

In the coming pages, we will explore ways to make this right response. We will hone our "worship" skills—that is, be more sensitive to the Lord's prompting and live more of our lives in a state of worship. It will mean the growth of our relationship with God, fulfilling the most important command given to us. It is the highest calling to which each of us may aspire.

chapter two

A Call to Worship
. . . but Where?

It is good to praise the LORD and make music to your name, O Most High, to proclaim your love in the morning and your faithfulness at night, to the music of the ten-stringed lyre and the melody of the harp.

Psalm 92:1–3

If we let our progress in religious life depend on the observance of externals alone, our devotion will quickly come to an end.

Thomas á Kempis

In the previous chapter, we found that two things must be present for one to worship the Lord. They are (1) a state I call "God-consciousness" and (2) our making a "right response" to this God-consciousness. Two steps, in that order. The nature of the first step is fairly easy to understand: We cannot be said to be worshiping God unless we are conscious of Him. In the course of this book, we will gain understanding about the second step; what, indeed, is our right response to God?

This question will be answered in part by exploring the two basic situations in which we worship the Lord. These are corporate worship—that is, times when we join with a group of fellow-believers at church, home, anywhere—and private worship—that is, times when we are alone with God.

Before we can start this exploration, however, we must first take a moment to understand a certain dichotomy about worship in our churches: We have more in common in our differences than we might realize.

Division? Or *Creative Variety?*

We begin with an important proposition: No two churches are alike. Not only are the worship services of various denominations different from one another, but each church within a given denomination can be different from all the rest.

Anyone who has ever moved from one town to another already knows this. While "shopping" for a new church, a part of you is constantly comparing the churches you visit to the one you just left. There never seems to be a church that is quite like the one in your old town. There never will be. They are all different.

This was even true in the early Church. A reading of Paul's letters gives us a variety of church styles, from Philippians to Galatians, from Corinthians to Colossians. Each had different strengths and weaknesses. The contrast is even greater among the seven churches from the book of Revelation (see Revelation 2–3).

Did you ever stop to think about the congregations in these various New Testament churches? How different they must have been, and how different their worship services might have been! Suppose one of the Ephesians traveled on business to Corinth and decided to go to the Christian church in town.

Doubtless he would have been delighted to find other believers who were worshiping together. But, as we are all prone to making comparisons, it is possible to imagine that he would have a few "unneighborly" thoughts going through his Ephesian head upon leaving the service: *That worship service certainly was longer than we have in Ephesus. Too long! . . . Why did they sing those strange, boring songs? . . . I wish they didn't use those modern Greek instruments.*

This supposition is not irreverence. The early saints were people, just like you and me. They, too, had their preferences concerning worship and when these were not used—remember, every church is different—they doubtless had just as much difficulty being patient and tolerant as we do.

Why are churches so different from one another? Don't we read the same Bible and pray to the same God? Certainly. Our differences arise from another factor: Churches are made up of *people.* Every person is unique and, therefore, every church will also be unique.

This seems to be fine with God, who, after all, is *very* creative. He inspired four different gospels, each of which tells the same life-changing story—but with distinct characteristics. He clearly accepts all types of people into His Kingdom—intelligent people, not-very-intelligent people, exciting people, boring people, nice people and, well, a number of grouchy, jerky people. I am sure you have met some of these individuals.

Knowing this to be true, we should not be surprised that there is such variety in churches and denominations—wild churches, dignified churches, churches that are very loud and churches that are rather quiet. After all, each church is made up of people—and some of these people are loud, others are quiet, etc.

God's Kingdom is large enough for a very diverse group of Christian churches. Consider His creativity at dispersing gifts and talents throughout His people: "There are different kinds of

45

gifts, but the same Spirit. There are different kinds of service, but the same Lord. There are different kinds of working, but the same God works all of them in all men" (1 Corinthians 12:4–6).

We can establish, therefore, that churches are different because people are different. But think about it from another angle. Do the differences in our churches signify *division* or simply *variety?*

You may well have heard a preacher rant and rave about the many "divisions" in the Body of Christ as they are disparagingly called. Indeed, non-Christians will refer to these "divisions" in an effort to mock Christianity and excuse their unbelief. Both cases involve unjust exaggeration.

Division comes at the point of disagreement about doctrine. And while it is true that doctrinal differences exist among various denominations, it is also true that for every obscure point we can find to argue about there are a hundred essential points on which we can all safely agree. As elucidated so well in C. S. Lewis's great work *Mere Christianity,* it is far better to concentrate on our commonalities than our controversies. The differences between any two denominations within Christianity are miniscule when compared with the difference between Christianity and anything else.

Therefore, we come to two important conclusions:

1. Every church is different—churches contain different people and therefore they will (and should!) be different in order to minister to those specific people. This is all right with God.
2. These differences are generally not as important, or as numerous, as those essential points that we have in common.

Yes, this could sound contradictory: Every church is different and every church has a great deal in common. Nevertheless, it is true. I have attended worship services in many different denominations and also in individual churches within denominations. The point we must realize is this: The actual differences in these groups of very different people seldom relate to doctrine; the differences are generally a matter of worship *styles*.

"What heresy!" shouts the minister of music reading this last sentence, understandably proud of the way his church worships. But think about it. One church may begin with a song, while another church begins with a prayer. Perhaps another begins with a word of exhortation, while still another begins with a Bible reading. These are differences in order, not content.

Some of the clergy don beautiful vestments, while others wear suits. I know of church services in which the leaders wear old blue jeans. In the same way, some church buildings are beautiful edifices in marble and stained glass, while others are simple and unadorned. But I ask you: Are these visual choices really important before the Lord? Let's hope not.

Doubtless the most obvious area of discord concerns music. Some church members sing older hymns; others sing contemporary songs. Some use organ, some synthesizer. Some add orchestral instruments, others add the drums and electric guitars of modern rock music. And yes, the music of some churches is quiet, while for others . . . *loud!*

Sometimes the musical preferences among various denominations are almost comical. I own a number of hymnals—the United Methodist Hymnal, the Baptist Hymnal and so on. A few songs are so universal (like *Amazing Grace*) as to be found in all the hymnals. Yet the editors often change the harmonization to make sure it "sounds" like the musical style of their own denomination—not someone else's!

Again, such differences are not doctrinal or scriptural; they are, in this case, *musical.* They simply exhibit different worship styles. (There is one major exception to this point of musical differences, which regards certain aspects of charismatic worship. This will be dealt with more fully in chapter 8.)

Most of us have strong feelings about these matters. If we are truly honest, however, we will recognize that these differences are not based on major theological or doctrinal variances. They are simply a question of style, of individual taste, of tradition, of "what you are comfortable with" or "used to."

This may not sit well with Christians who have been taught that their church or denomination is "right" and all the others are wrong. Maybe the Ephesians thought that about the Galatians and Philippians. Paul did not think so, and I suggest that our Lord does not either.

The biblical injunction given throughout the fourteenth chapter of Romans clearly forbids us to censure another Christian church on such debatable matters as worship styles: "Therefore let us stop passing judgment on one another" (Romans 14:13). One is reminded of a maxim of Augustine: "In essential matters, unity; in debatable matters, liberty; in all things, charity."

This is not to ridicule any tradition or liturgy. God uses these distinctions to meet us where we are and bring us to Himself. But the same God can be worshiped in both "high" churches and "low" churches. He seems to like both. The differences in worship styles among all these churches do not bother our Lord—perhaps they should not bother us either.

Sunday Morning: What Is Happening?

We have established that the differences in the various churches' modes of worship are not as profound as might appear at first glance. Let us begin, then, to understand a right response to God in worship by looking at the "corporate worship" portion of our Sunday morning services (with apologies to Seventh Day Adventists who, of course, worship on Saturday).

Think back to last Sunday at your church. Do you remember the corporate worship? What was happening at that time?

You may answer on several levels. At the very least, you may recall the name of a song you sang with your congregation. Perhaps you remember how the song leader or minister of music looked on the platform. Better still, maybe you can remember a spiritual insight or inspiration that occurred at the time.

For those of you who do not remember anything from last Sunday's service, bring any time of corporate worship to mind. Do you have it in memory now? Good. Now consider: What is happening at such a time?

Probably a number of things are occurring simultaneously:

- some may be singing praise—that is, acclaiming the wonderful attributes of God;
- some may be praying, talking to God, perhaps entreating Him for their needs;
- some may be listening quietly for God's direction and guidance;
- some may be meditating on God's Word, pondering the wisdom of the Lord;
- some may be speaking aloud to God or shouting praises.

This list could also go on and on. Of course, other things are going on as well. A teenage girl is rummaging through her purse. Two young siblings are pinching each other while their parents are singing away, oblivious. A man in a suit slips a pocket calendar out of his jacket and jots down a few notes. An exasperated mother is holding her little boy tightly while shaking a finger in his guilty-looking face. For the purposes of this book, we will ignore these inevitable activities and concentrate on the spiritual side of your Sunday morning service.

What Brings Us Together?

Ministers often like to quote Hebrews 10:25, in which the writer admonishes us not to "give up meeting together." The ministers are right to remind us of this, for it is an important command of Scripture and should be a major factor in our growth as Christians. But have you ever wondered why God wants us to do so?

To begin with, it is obviously a good thing for our souls to hear the Gospel preached and to be exhorted in the teachings of

the Bible. Certainly it is good for us to be encouraged by standing collectively with other believers. Among other things, it
reminds us, à la Elijah, that we are not "the only one left," and
that God has many others who have not "bowed the knee to
Baal." And, of course, it is fitting that we should perform other
Sunday morning actions: celebrating holy Communion as a
"remembrance of Christ," giving alms for the poor and to support the clergy, etc.

But this book is about worship, not church attendance. So I
ask: Why would God want us *to gather together* to worship Him?
Specifically, why would He want us to gather together to sing
about Him (and to Him) when we could do so just as well at
home? To understand this we need to look at two particular elements involved in worship.

God put within each person an inborn love of music (at least,
some form of music) and a natural appreciation of beauty and
order. Now I am not suggesting that we all frequent symphony
halls and art galleries. I mean simply that most of us like music
of a certain kind and that each of us desires a certain beauty and
orderliness about us.

If you feel inclined to argue against this second point, let me
ask you: Do you like delicious food or burnt food? Do you prefer fresh air or smog? Would you rather drive a new car or an old
clunker that barely runs? I ask these somewhat silly questions to
illustrate what I mean when I claim that we all appreciate—at
least in some manner—beauty and orderliness. And this applies
to our worship as well.

An important scriptural command links our worship of God
with this inborn love of beauty: Worship the Lord in the beauty
of His holiness. To emphasize the significance of this concept—
that beauty comes directly from Him—this phrase is found in
the Bible, not once or twice, but four times: 1 Chronicles 16:29;
2 Chronicles 20:21; Psalm 29:2; and Psalm 96:9.

This is the meaning behind King David's desire to "gaze upon
the beauty of the LORD" (Psalm 27:4). Not only does all beauty

come from Him, but our natural appreciation of it also comes from Him. This is also why Paul exhorts us: "Whatever is true, whatever is noble, whatever is right, whatever is pure, whatever is *lovely*, whatever is admirable—if anything is excellent or praiseworthy— think about such things" (Philippians 4:8, emphasis added).

Throughout the ages, Christians have appreciated "the beauty of the Lord," and how the beauty found in nature comes from God. Augustine, in the *Confessions*, called the Lord "My Father, O Beauty of all things beautiful." God utilizes our love of music and beauty to help us find ways to worship Him as we should.

Some of you may not agree with this. If you are one, I ask you to consider the following conversation on this subject that I once had with a friend from my church who has a passion for corporate worship. She insisted, "No, it has nothing to do with the music itself. I am simply caught up in the flow of the *spirit* of worship."

The following Sunday I was playing the piano during our time of corporate worship. It was an excellent service and the entire congregation (including my friend) certainly seemed to be "caught up in the flow of the spirit of worship." That is, until I stupidly lost my concentration and hit a resoundingly wrong chord. It was like dropping a bomb on the church. Everyone stopped singing and turned in dismay to the red-faced piano player. My friend, standing nearby, saw me and burst out laughing.

But the point was clear: Worship *did* involve the music, and the beauty of it. When the beauty ceased with that dissonant sound, the worship ceased as well.

God wants us to desire Him, to spend time with Him, to fellowship with Him. He also knows that, since the Fall of man, we do not naturally have a very strong inclination to do this. So He solved the riddle by placing within us this love of music and beauty, using them like an inner magnet to draw us into corporate worship.

The Role of the "Introducer"

So we can see that our innate love of music and beauty is given to us by God for a purpose, that it is to be an aid in corporate worship. Now let's look more closely at how this works.

You will recall from the previous chapter that I compared the beginning of God-consciousness to the beginning of a conversation. Either person could start it. I also mentioned a possible "third party" who could introduce the two people who then begin the conversation. Let us examine this concept further.

Suppose there is someone in your neighborhood whom you have casually met, but who really seems to admire you and wants to get to know you. We will give him the name Jim. Unfortunately, you are terribly busy at this time of your life and have little inclination for extra social activities. Perhaps Jim has called you occasionally and you chatted politely for a while but did not take up the hints he left for "getting together sometime."

Most people would probably abandon the effort after such a rebuff, but Jim is undaunted. He enlists the aid of a third party, Bill, who is already your good friend. This third party asks you to come over to his house when Jim is also there. Bill initiates a game that all three of you can play. He encourages conversation between you and Jim. In this atmosphere, you find yourself getting to know Jim—and you eventually establish a strong friendship.

In this analogy, Jim represents the place of God Himself. He loves us and longs to spend time in fellowship with us but we are, by our fallen nature, not *naturally* enthusiastic about the idea. Many Scriptures testify to this sad truth: "There is no one righteous, not even one; there is no one who understands, no one who seeks God" (Romans 3:10–11). Furthermore, our world constantly pressures us to stay as busy as possible. (It does not seem to matter what you are busy doing, as long as you are really busy. Or so our world tells us.)

But God is not easily put off—for which we can be very thankful. Like the relentless pursuer in Francis Thompson's powerful poem *The Hound of Heaven,* God is determined to find a way to get our attention. Knowing that we have an inborn love of music and appreciation of beauty and order (remember that He was the Creator who put these things in us—and for this very reason), God employs such "third parties" as music to woo us to Himself. We come into a worship service, our minds preoccupied with a thousand cares. Though we may be physically present at church, mentally we are too busy to bother with God.

Then we see our Christian friends and the music begins. If we abandon ourselves to the flow of these wonderful externals and begin to sing, pray and "set our minds on things above," something happens. When we sing God's praises in a fine song with skillful accompaniment, when we marvel at the beauty of our churches (architecture, banners, vestments), when we are moved by beautiful and meaningful prayers—God uses these external motivators in order to open the way for something internal to happen. A worship experience with other believers has led to an internal, intimate time of communion: a private worship experience.

Why does God desire corporate worship? This is why.

When Aids Become Idols

For centuries the Lord has used this natural inclination toward music and beauty in a wide variety of external tools to bring us closer to Him through corporate gatherings. He has used lofty cathedrals, whose architecture attracts our gaze toward heaven. He has used liturgies, incense and vestments to create theatrical scenes of otherworldly drama—whatever each of us appreciates and feels is our own—to attract us.

Since the Fall, we find that we need such "aids to worship." (Incidentally, you will notice that before the Fall, such externals were unnecessary. Adam and Eve had free communion with God, and there is no hint of needing a tabernacle, a temple, a synagogue or a church. Certainly the innocently unclad duo would have wondered at the reason for vestments!)

And of course, there is nothing wrong with this, any more than with our present need for clothing—another consequence of the Fall. It would be foolish not to recognize our obvious needs and just as foolish to scorn *any* aid that helps us draw closer to the Lord.

If we accept that these wonderful externals act as "introducer" between us and God, then we need to examine further what this role is and what it is not. When someone introduces two people, the three of them will visit together for a certain time. Yet if the introducer is faithfully fulfilling his or her role and truly wants the two parties to get to know one another, there comes a time to leave them alone. This is like a good hostess who instinctively takes her cue to make a graceful exit. In the old romantic movies the line was, "I'll let you two get better acquainted."

Without this step, the two never will get better acquainted. There is a very different dynamic between a threesome and a twosome. Many things, certainly many intimate things, will never be shared in a group setting. As the saying goes, "Two's company; three's a crowd."

To use a different analogy: a young woman may use her external beauty to woo a young man toward her. This is very natural. Once a relationship begins, if it is to mature, the couple will move beyond the initial physical attraction into deeper topics: their personalities, their common likes and dislikes, their aspirations and dreams. Indeed, for a successful marriage to blossom and endure, the couple had better progress far beyond the fleeting charms of physical beauty.

In the same way the musical instruments, the songs, the stained-glass windows—whatever helps us enter into God-consciousness—are all good things. There comes a time, though, when they can actually get in the way. Anything that is supposed to serve as a means to a higher end gets in the way when it becomes an end in itself.

Perhaps a particular song has the ability to draw you closer to the Lord. Sing it, by all means! Let it bring you to God in worship. But if the end of the song is also the end of the worship, something is wrong. Your attention has been captured not by God whom the introducer—the song—has brought you to, but by the introducer itself.

This is the inherent danger of all aids to worship, no matter how good in themselves they may be. Unless we use them properly they can become the objects of our affection instead of God. This is why even such an exalted act as partaking in corporate worship can actually become a distraction from God, even an idol.

This type of idolatry was clearly defined by Martin Luther when he pointed out: "Whatever your heart clings to and confides in is really your God." This is why it is actually possible to love the trappings of worship—to love the music, the praying, the feelings of exultation—more than we love the God we are attempting to worship.

You might point out that such idolatry could also occur in private worship. This is true. Let's go back to the idea that a particular song can greatly enhance your worship time. When the song has concluded, you may or may not continue your communion with the Lord. In fact, it is a benefit of worship in a corporate setting that outside stimuli will beckon to you to continue to worship—a new song, a word from the pastor, a public prayer. Any of these may refocus your attention back to God, a benefit that is harder to come by in private worship. By the same token, there are more "aids" to become idols in a corporate setting.

Aids to worship are good when they bring us to God and then get out of the way. Any element of corporate—or private—worship becomes an idol when it focuses our attention on itself.

The "Privacy" of Worship

We need to make an important differentiation at this point. Look at these two statements about the external/internal experience as we are drawn into corporate worship:

1. In all worship, God and people meet and commune on various spiritual levels. We talked about how music and beauty act as "introducers" leading us to God-consciousness. Whatever the means of introduction, the worshipers became aware of the Lord and made a right response—as we discussed in the previous chapter.
2. In each case, with each worshiper, nothing is happening that could not take place when he or she is alone in the privacy of his or her own home.

"What do you mean?" some may remonstrate. "We don't have pipe organs in our houses. Nor could we fit entire congregations into our living rooms!"

Remember, the pipe organs (or whatever musical instruments your church uses or avoids), the liturgy, the choir robes, even the minister are external stimulants God uses to prod us—gently or forcibly—back to Himself. They are means to a higher end; they are not the end itself. They are *aids* to worship, but they are not worship. These things are externals and one can have external aids to worship in a private setting just as easily as in a group setting. God wants something internal to happen, and each person who is truly worshiping—either in a group or alone—is internally involved in the two steps established in the first chapter for worship to take place: God-consciousness and the right reaction to it.

Recall the instruction that God gave to Samuel when he had been sent to anoint the young David as king over Israel: "The LORD does not look at the things man looks at. Man looks at the outward appearance, but the LORD looks at the heart" (1 Samuel 16:7).

Therefore, having praised the concept of corporate worship, we come to some rather uncomfortable conclusions about it. God does not seem to care much about how gorgeous your voice is, or how lovely your sanctuary is, or how stirring your music is, or how eloquent your song leader is. God wants *your heart*. He wants the heart of each individual worshiper.

This simple but profound revelation appears again and again throughout church history. In the classic devotional *The Imitation of Christ,* Thomas á Kempis warns us: "If we let our progress in religious life depend on the observance of externals alone, our devotion will quickly come to an end." One great worshiper, Anselm of Canterbury, who lived in the eleventh century, gave his heart to Christ and prayed to God from the depths of his soul: "O Lord our God, grant us grace to desire Thee with our whole heart, that, so desiring, we may seek, and seeking find Thee, and so finding Thee may love Thee, and loving Thee, may hate those sins from which Thou hast redeemed us."

In his excellent book *Let us Praise,* Judson Cornwall, truly an expert in leading corporate worship, made the following observation: "Praise is not a mass function. It is the response of an individual to his God. When a group of individuals chooses to unite in praising, their individual responses may blend into a group response, but every expression of the praise comes from a separate individual."

Take a moment to look at your Sunday morning service. What do you see? You see a group, a congregation involved in corporate worship. God sees each individual heart, whether it is turned toward Him or preoccupied with trying to "out-sing" his neighbor. As hearts respond, as participants become deeply involved in worshiping their Lord, we find that this is in reality a roomful of "private" worshipers. Ultimately it is this worship, the internal communion in the privacy of one's heart, that should be brought into our private worship times and, indeed, into every aspect of our lives.

So, Is One Better than the Other?

By now some of you may be objecting on the grounds that I seem to be opposed to corporate worship: "Isn't corporate worship something wonderful that the Bible clearly commands? Doesn't Psalm 22 say that God inhabits the praises of His people?"

Yes, this is one of His many promises. God is present when His people are praising Him, but He is just as present when only one of His people is praising Him. If, for instance, I begin to sing praise to Him in my quiet time each day, do you think He will shut His ears unless I gather some friends to sing harmony with me?

I desire in no way to pit corporate worship against private worship or vice versa. Nor am I arguing that one is more important or more effective than the other. That is like trying to argue which of the two blades of your scissors is the more important. Corporate worship and private worship are both critical to our spiritual growth and to deepening our relationship with the Lord. Both are found in, and encouraged by, the Scriptures.

Nevertheless, one purpose of this book is to correct the disproportionate emphasis given to corporate worship over private worship in the church today. To many Christians, worship means corporate worship. That is, they speak of worship as something that happens in a church (or "home church") setting. I am afraid that many—they might not want to admit this—even equate worship with "singing Christian songs." Is this all that worship is?

I have led God's people in praise and worship for over two decades. Certainly I know the immeasurable worth of corporate worship. Yet the more I experience it, the more I am convinced that the need of the hour is not corporate worship, but private worship—the need for each Christian to spend time every day alone with God in worship.

The renowned Daniel Webster summed this feeling up in one sentence: "The most important thought I ever had was that of my *individual* responsibility to God." The Lord sees His people not as a homogenized mass but as individual souls who relate personally with their Creator. Therefore, our worship must be personal as well.

Yet in the dozens of books and pamphlets I have read that promote a daily quiet time with God, virtually none even introduces the subject of private worship. That is, current teaching about having daily devotions seldom encourages us to engage in worship of the Lord—much less without others, without music, without praying, without even a Bible.

Does it surprise us to read that the majority of times when people are worshiping God in the pages of Scripture, they do so *without these things?* (More on this in the next two chapters.)

These books encourage prayer and reading the Word—two absolutely essential elements of our Christian life. With all my heart and soul I recommend them to you. But again we must consider the "why" behind these actions: Do we read Scripture so that we can become notable Bible scholars, or in order to get to know the Author of the book? Do we pray so that we can importune God to give us all we need, or in order to have fellowship with our greatest and dearest Friend?

Which "Charges You Up" More?

What answers do you give to these questions? Here is a suggestion to help you discern what you really believe. Let's assume that you went to church last Sunday. (Perhaps you were sick or out of town or just feeling lazy. But let's assume you were there.) Suppose someone approached you after the service and asked with sincerity, "Why did you go to church today?"

Let us also suppose that you were absolutely honest with your answers. Perhaps you explained how much you love your church, your pastor and your Christian friends. This is a most excellent answer. Or perhaps you admitted that you were simply going to church out of obedience. This might not be a very joyful answer but it is still valid, as there is much in the Bible about obedience—doing good things because they should be done, whether you feel like doing them or not.

Suppose the interrogater went deeper: "What *need* do you have that is met by going to your church?" Typically the answer could be summed up in the common expression: "I need to have my batteries recharged."

Let's look at what this is really saying. Now nothing is wrong with such an admission. Our Lord does not rebuke us for this. Indeed, Jesus said, "Come to me, all you who are weary and burdened, and I will give you rest" (Matthew 11:28). Anyone living and working in today's high-stress, secular society has felt his or her batteries ebbing at times. And it would be a fool who, knowing that his batteries are low, refuses to go to a place where they can be recharged.

The point of my using this analogy is simply to point out that *the Battery Charger is always available*—not just at church!

My wife and I used to own an old car that was difficult to start on a cold winter's morning. I know very little about cars and batteries, but someone told me to buy an inexpensive home battery charger, which I did. On some mornings this gave enough power to get the old car started, but on the coldest days I had to call the service station for help. Soon (well, not very soon) a large truck would arrive, park next to our car, hook up some thick cables and start the car. I assume that their battery charger was more powerful than our little one.

Similarly, we look to our church services to jump-start our walks with God. We concede that our private worship times are helpful and we try to have them when we can find the time. But those times of *corporate* worship, well, they really boost up the batteries as nothing else can, right?

This is a faulty view of both the church and our personal relationship to God. It is true that we should be faithful church members, but not for the purpose of charging our internal batteries. That is something that can take place between God and you anytime, anywhere. We go to church to serve, to encourage others, to learn to be better equipped in our faith—for a thousand wonderful and valid reasons—but not to recharge weak batteries. At least, this should be only an exception, not the rule.

To view churchgoing as a battery-charging opportunity is actually to put the church service between you and God Himself. It is to make the means an end. Why should we want to do this? Why would you ever want to put anything between you and your Lord?

The Daily Availability of Worship

I hope that no ministers of music reading this are becoming uneasy about job security. The fears may speak something like this: "If churchgoers started spending time each day in private worship, why would they need to come together to worship at all? Wouldn't this put me out of a job?"

Not to worry! The exact opposite is true. Those saints who spend time privately worshiping the Lord also become more and more hungry for corporate worship. It is a food that both meets our appetites and whets them for more. As Brother Lawrence points out in *The Practice of the Presence of God*, "The more one knows him, the more one wants to know him."

A parallel case could be made for daily Bible reading. Many years ago I had a conversation with a pastor on the subject of his preaching. Although he preached the Gospel and gave many excellent sermons from the Word, he admitted that he had never specifically mentioned that his congregation should read the Bible throughout the week.

When I asked him why not, he gave a few hesitant answers. Finally he laughed and said, "If they read the Bible all week, why would they show up on Sunday to hear about it from me?" He seemed to be joking, but I wondered if that was a real fear.

If so, he need not have worried. Those who study the Scriptures on their own are those who listen with the most eagerness on Sunday morning. Indeed, they are the best prepared to hear, as they come to the service already "warmed up." A hunger for God's Word is a passion one can never fully meet. There is always a taste for more.

The same is true of worship. This is why the psalmist commands: "Sing to the LORD, praise his name; proclaim his salvation *day after day*" (Psalm 96:2, emphasis added). He does not say, "Proclaim his salvation on some days" or "on the Sabbath day." Worship is to be daily, not weekly.

The eminent statesman Dag Hammarskjöld (who became Secretary General of the United Nations from 1953 until his death in 1961) knew the value of worshiping God every day. He wrote that, "We die on the day when our lives cease to be illuminated by the steady radiance, renewed daily of a wonder—the source of which is beyond all reason." It is the radiance of the Lord—*renewed daily*—that is the authentic "recharger" of our batteries.

Most of us know that we should pray every day and that we should read the Bible on our own. Many of us memorize and meditate upon Scripture, and many are involved in steadfast intercessory prayer—not just at church but in our homes. And certainly we know that we are to be faithful witnesses for Christ during the week—in our offices, in our neighborhoods, wherever.

Yet for most of us, the time for worshiping the Lord is only at church, in the company of others.

For those of you who want to change this in your own lives and to enter an entirely new dimension in your relationship with the Lord, I invite you to read on.

chapter three

Corporate Worship
in the Bible

Then I heard every creature in heaven and on earth and under the earth and on the sea, and all that is in them, singing: "To him who sits on the throne and to the Lamb be praise and honor and glory and power, for ever and ever!"

Revelation 5:13

Therefore by your concord and harmonious love Jesus Christ is being sung. Now all of you together become a choir so that being harmoniously in concord and receiving the key note from God in unison you may sing with one voice through Jesus Christ to the Father.

Ignatius, Bishop of Antioch

When one writes a book, it is impossible to know the backgrounds of all the readers. Some may be new Christians while others have been in the faith for decades. For readers who have spent hours in the Bible and are quite familiar with the many Scriptures about worship, you may want to skip the next two chapters. As C. S. Lewis points out in *Mere Christianity*, "It is a very silly idea that in reading a book you must never 'skip.' All sensible people skip freely when they come to a chapter which they find is going to be of no use to them." So, if you are already familiar with the examples of worship in the Bible—unless, of course, you would like a refresher—feel free to proceed to chapter five.

Let's begin, then, with a general note. A great many biblical passages concern worship, both in corporate and private settings. It might be helpful as you read them to remember that all the worship passages fall into one of two broad categories: *examples* or *exhortations*. That is, either the passage gives us a historical example of people worshiping God, or the passage simply exhorts or commands us to worship.

An "example" of corporate worship from the Old Testament, for instance, is found in Ezra 3:11: "With praise and thanksgiving they sang to the LORD: 'He is good; his love to Israel endures forever.' And all the people gave a great shout of praise to the LORD, because the foundation of the house of the LORD was laid."

An "exhortation" from the Old Testament, applicable to either corporate or private worship, is found in Psalm 100:2. It does not give us any historical scene; rather, it commands us to "worship the LORD with gladness; come before him with joyful songs." As you may suspect, the book of Psalms contains the majority of these biblical "exhortations."

In the New Testament, "examples" are generally found in the historical narratives such as the gospels and the book of Acts—not to mention Revelation—and "exhortations" are found usually (but not exclusively) in letters from Paul, John and others.

It should also be mentioned that our two-chapter study will not cover every verse concerning worship, praise or other related subjects. That would be a book in itself! If you have a good concordance or a Bible computer program, you can look up supplementary verses. For our purposes it will suffice to explore key Scriptures and consider how they might inspire us to greater worship.

We reasoned in the previous chapter that nothing happens internally in individuals in corporate worship that could not happen in the privacy of their own homes. We saw further how today's church greatly overemphasizes the role of corporate worship while placing little emphasis on an individual Christian's private worship time. Let's begin to examine in this chapter on corporate worship and the next on private worship what we can learn from Scripture.

The Basis of Worship Today

It may startle Christians to learn that the typical Sunday morning worship of today is modeled more on "examples" from the Old Testament than the New. That is partly because more biblical examples of groups of people worshiping God are found in the Old Testament; there is little in the New Testament for us to copy. But there is a more significant explanation.

The experiences of corporate worship in the New Testament were not newly designed formats; they were modeled after worship experiences of the Old Testament. This should not surprise us. The earliest Christians were Jews, deeply immersed in the Hebrew worship traditions. The early Christian church services were directly related to those of the Jewish Synagogue: readings from Scripture, congregational singing, teaching by the leaders and so on.

One of the practical applications of Matthew 5:17, where Jesus said, "Do not think that I have come to abolish the Law or the Prophets; I have not come to abolish them but to fulfill them," is that of the church service. In a manner of speaking, the first "Christian Worship Service" was the Last Supper where holy Communion was initiated. Yet this event was in the context of the long-established Passover meal, and the hymn that Christ and His disciples sang (see Matthew 26:30) was likely from the Hillel—Hebrew songs of praise from the Psalms.

Ultimately, the Christian church service itself has an extended history that begins in the first book of the Bible. The progression, beginning with Genesis 4:26 when "men began to call on the name of the LORD," could be outlined as follows.

1. *Altars are used to honor God:* "Then Noah built an altar to the Lord" (Genesis 8:20). Although this is the first mention of an altar, some scholars believe they were in use before Noah.
2. *The Tabernacle and Ark of the Covenant are built to receive God's presence:* "Then have them make a sanctuary for me, and I will dwell among them. Make this tabernacle and all its furnishings exactly like the pattern I will show you" (Exodus 25:8–9).
3. *The Temple stands as a "permanent" house for the Ark:* "Solomon gave orders to build a temple for the Name of the LORD" (2 Chronicles 2:1).
4. *Synagogues offer a gathering place for local worshipers:* "He went to Nazareth, where he had been brought up, and on the Sabbath day he went into the synagogue, as was his custom" (Luke 4:16). The synagogue tradition actually began much earlier during the centuries between the writings of the Old and New Testaments, or perhaps as far back as the Babylonian captivity.
5. *Christian church services are held in the remains of the Temple:* "And all the believers used to meet together in Solomon's Colonnade" (Acts 5:12);
   -then in homes: "Greet also the church that meets at their house" (Romans 16:5);
   -and later in church buildings. This would not happen until long after the New Testament was written.

A number of observations could be made from this progression from altars to churches. The ones that concern us are:

1. Each stage in the progression was for the purpose of making the participants more God-conscious. The elements of the "worship services" existed so that God's people might be reminded of Him and drawn to Him.
2. Each stage in the progression involved externals, including animal sacrifices on altars, the contents of the Ark of the Covenant, singing and incense in the Temple, scrolls in the synagogue and the love feasts of the early Church. Each of these externals existed to encourage something *internal* within the individual participants: the worship of the Lord.

Corporate Worship in the Old Testament

What can we learn from looking at corporate worship in the Bible? Is this simply an interesting history lesson that has little application for us today? In his letter to the Romans, Paul quotes extensively from the Old Testament and gives us the ultimate reason for it: "For everything that was written in the past was written to teach us, so that through endurance and the encouragement of the Scriptures we might have hope" (Romans 15:4).

In order to relate these worship scenes to our topic, I will comment about how these passages help us to worship our Lord. Most of the "lessons" that we will study are interpretive rather than literal. It is when we dig deep to answer the "why" questions that we find the meaning that can help us today.

Take, for instance, the Sabbath. The Old Testament gave specific commands regarding the Sabbath, but Jesus had to correct His people's overly literal interpretation. It had become little more than an elaborate game of rule-following. Jesus brought us back to the "why" of the Sabbath: It was given to us that we might have rest, have regular time devoted to worship and prayer, have a special time to draw close to God—not to figure out how many ounces we could legally carry for so many yards.

Therefore, as we consider scriptural passages we will ask, "What is in this passage that I could learn from and apply toward my worship of God?" We are not studying the Bible to become scholars but to change our lives.

The "examples" of corporate worship recorded in the Old Testament fall into five general categories: thanksgiving, warfare, feasts, celebration and dedications (the Temple, the wall of Jerusalem, etc.). Without covering an exhaustive list, let us consider the primary "examples" of each category.

Thanksgiving

One of the most famous "praise services" in the Bible was not planned beforehand. It sprang from the people's gratitude for God's miraculous protection. This took place immediately after the parting of the Red Sea, and it is recorded in the first 21 verses of Exodus 15: "Sing to the LORD, for he is highly exalted. The horse and its rider he has hurled into the sea" (Exodus 15:21).

The key word to this glorious scene in Israel's history is *spontaneous* thanksgiving. Although Moses was himself a participant, we do not assume that he instigated this time of worship. He could not have controlled it if he had tried! Who can say how it began, and whether the people (all of them?) sang together or if every voice simply added to the joyful cacophony. (Certainly it took Holy Spirit inspiration to write it all down afterward!) It involved both instruments and dancing (verse 20), and its beauty was not in careful preparation and rehearsal but in irrepressible and ecstatic abandonment to God.

What can we learn from this passage? Many things—indeed, dozens of sermons have been preached from this text. For our purposes, the main insight to be noted is this: Our response when something wonderful happens should be immediate praise to God.

All of us have had unexpected good things come our way. Perhaps they are answers to our prayers; perhaps they are completely unsought. What is our reaction to such blessings? It should be praise and, most importantly, *immediate* praise. The Israelites did not take time to schedule and plan an elaborate worship service. They simply exploded with praise for the God who saved them.

This is the type of thanksgiving that is described so well by E. M. Bounds in his classic, *Possibilities of Prayer:* "The radiance and gratitude and utterance of thanksgiving must be there. This is not simply the poetry of praise, but the deep-toned words and prose of thanks. There must be hardy thanks, which remembers the past, sees God in it, and voices that recognition in sincere thanksgiving."

The words *thank you* are wonderful to hear. How every mother longs to hear her children say "Thank you" for cooking a delicious meal (among countless other things)! How sad it would be to never hear those words, and how delightful when they come without delay! This should be our immediate response to our Lord for every special blessing sent to us from Him. And they *all* come from Him: "Every good and perfect gift is from above, coming down from the Father . . ." (James 1:17).

Warfare

A tremendous showing of the spiritual power of worship is given in the twentieth chapter of 2 Chronicles. A strong army was about to attack Judah and King Jehoshaphat knew that his people were in danger of being annihilated. He called for a time of prayer and fasting. After hearing God's direction through one of the Levites and then consulting the people, he took an unusual action.

Jehoshaphat appointed men to sing to the LORD and to praise him for the splendor of his holiness as they went out at the head of the army, saying: "Give thanks to the LORD, for his love endures forever." As they began to sing and praise, the LORD set ambushes against the men of Ammon and Moab and Mount Seir who were invading Judah, and they were defeated.

2 Chronicles 20:21–22

69

The twofold lesson here is the counterpart to the Red Sea passage. When terrible, unexpected news comes to you, two needs arise immediately: (1) time to seek the Lord for His answer to the situation and (2) time to praise God. We all know that this can be dreadfully difficult, but it releases power on our behalf in the larger struggle of life. As Paul explains: "For our struggle is not against flesh and blood, but against the rulers, against the authorities, against the powers of this dark world and against the spiritual forces of evil in the heavenly realms" (Ephesians 6:12).

Is this difficult to believe in our practical, businesslike world? Of course it is, particularly when one is in a stressful time of need. But it is true nonetheless. Doubtless it was difficult for his soldiers to believe that Jehoshaphat's "musical artillery" would work. (One can easily imagine some of the uneasy glances of the warriors who were not yet convinced.)

Who knows what prayers and praise filled the heart of King Jehoshaphat in the time of faith-testing? Perhaps his words were like those given by Thomas á Kempis in *The Imitation of Christ* during a time of trial:

> Just Father, ever to be praised, the hour has come for your servant to be tried. Beloved Father, it is right that in this hour your servant should suffer something for you. O Father, forever to be honored, the hour which you knew from all eternity is at hand, when for a short time your servant should be outwardly oppressed, but inwardly should ever live with you.

This type of "praise under pressure" is what the letter to the Hebrews calls "a *sacrifice* of praise" (Hebrews 13:15, emphasis added). A sacrifice always costs us something. It is a giving away of what we want to keep. It is inherently difficult. So it is during those times when we are in trouble, despair or discouragement that we must discipline our wills to bring praise to God. This sacrifice of praise is perhaps our most powerful weapon of spiritual warfare. It can produce the type of miraculous turnabouts that Jehoshaphat and his army ultimately experienced.

Feasts

Three principal feasts were celebrated in the Jewish year, as summarized in Deuteronomy 16:16: "Three times a year all your men must appear before the LORD your God at the place he will choose: at the Feast of Unleavened Bread [that is, the Passover], the Feast of Weeks [that is, Pentecost] and the Feast of Tabernacles." The twenty-third chapter of Leviticus adds the Feast of Trumpets (verse 24) and the Day of Atonement (verse 27). One other regular "feast" should also be considered, one that relates directly to our present-day church services. This is the Sabbath, the weekly gathering of believers, "a day of rest, a holy Sabbath to the LORD" (Exodus 16:23).

Each of these feast days has its own special significance along with individual ordinances, ceremonies and customs. All of them require offerings to the Lord, and all of them involve a Sabbath-like time in which the Israelites are to "do no regular work" (Leviticus 23:25).

We could explore many insights in each of these Old Testament feast days, but the basic concept we want to note is this: *regularity*. We need to be regular, not sporadic, in our worship of the Lord.

It is not as though God wants "clock watchers" among His people—those who carefully worship at certain times or on all special days like Sunday (but not on other days). Through these feasts He is teaching His people to take on worship as a lifestyle. And the way that this lifestyle is learned is through regularity, through worshiping every day, not just when we feel like it.

Worship benefits the soul's relationship to God somewhat similarly to the way vitamins benefit the body. Would you neglect to take your daily vitamin, and then take a handful of them once each week? Of course not. Vitamins work if taken regularly. The same is true of worship. We were not made to go six days without worshiping and then try to cram in a week's worth of it on Sunday! We were made to worship God each day of our lives.

Celebration

The Jewish people have endured many grievous and sorrowful times in their long history. Yet when their fortunes improve, they know how to celebrate with a joy that is unbounded. One of the best examples occurred when King David brought the Ark of the Covenant into Jerusalem. The jubilant story is told in two parallel passages: 2 Samuel 6:12–23 and the much longer account in 1 Chronicles 15–16.

There were extensive preparations, including the consecration of the Levites and the appointing of specific instrumentalists (lyres, harps, cymbals, rams' horns and trumpets) and singers (choirs). On the great day when the Ark was brought to Jerusalem with great musical accompaniment, David "danced before the LORD with all his might, while he and the entire house of Israel brought up the ark of the LORD with shouts and the sound of trumpets" (2 Samuel 6:14–15). Afterward, in order to establish continual praise before the Ark, David appointed certain musicians to work there daily. He gave them a beautiful psalm of thanks (1 Chronicles 16:8–36), and made them "responsible for the sounding of the trumpets and cymbals and for the playing of the other instruments for sacred song" (1 Chronicles 16:42).

David's exuberant worship is an important illustration for us. He "danced before the Lord *with all his might.*" In a similar sense of celebration, our worship of God must be wholehearted, not halfhearted. We are called to praise God with our whole selves, with *enthusiasm;* the word comes from the Greek phrase "to be inspired by God." As Emerson reminds us, "Nothing great was ever achieved without enthusiasm." And we want to produce great praise to the Lord, as David did.

In the case of corporate worship, a good minister of music always tries to be sensitive to the exuberance (or lack of it) throughout the congregation. He can usually tell if the people are entering into the worship with complete abandon or if they are somewhat grudgingly mouthing the words. Certainly different personality types come into play here, as well as one's circumstances. (More on this topic in chapter 6.) But whatever our personalities and whatever our circumstances, we need to take what we have and offer it wholeheartedly to the Lord.

In this respect, worship is a form of *giving*, giving ourselves completely to God. In fact, the same admonitions about giving our money apply to giving ourselves in worship: "Each man should give what he has decided in his heart to give, *not reluctantly or under compulsion*, for God loves a cheerful giver" (2 Corinthians 9:7, emphasis added). In the same way, our worship— corporate or private—must never be given "reluctantly or under compulsion." Instead, we should feel free to worship the Lord "with all our might," knowing that God joyfully accepts such an offering of exuberant praise.

Dedication

Perhaps the best known of the corporate worship experiences of the Old Testament are from the category of dedications. These include the dedication of Solomon's Temple (2 Chronicles 5:1–7:10), the purification of the Temple by Hezekiah (2 Chronicles 29:3–36), the dedication of Nehemiah's wall around Jerusalem (Nehemiah 12:27–43), and the dedication of the Second Temple and of its foundation (Ezra 3:11–13).

Each passage contains inspiring verses, and each contains insights about worshiping the Lord. For purposes of illustration, let us choose the story in Ezra mentioned earlier of the dedication of the second Temple's foundation, after the Babylonian captivity. A ceremony, held when the foundation was laid, included instrumentalists and singers from among the Levites. After their time of worship, the people responded: "And all the people gave a great shout of praise to the LORD, because the foundation of the house of the LORD was laid" (Ezra 3:11).

The common point in this passage with the other dedication stories is this: *beginning something new*. When the Israelites had a new Temple, or even a new wall, they understood the importance of dedicating it to the Lord. They realized how critical it

73

is to start something in the right direction, knowing that anything askew initially will only worsen in the coming years.

In the same way, whenever we face a new beginning in our lives, we need to dedicate ourselves anew to God in worship. The turning points of our lives—whether they be marriage, children, a new job, a change of schools or any major decisions—must be completely given over to the Lord from the outset. Again, this class of worship is not something that should wait for a Sunday service. It is part of our day-to-day worship experience with the Lord.

But why *worship* at these times? Certainly one can see the need for fervent prayer in crucial times of life, or extra time studying the Scriptures. But worship?

The answer lies in the area of faith: "being sure of what we hope for and certain of what we do not see" (Hebrews 11:1). When we begin something new in our lives with worship, we release our faith in God's blessing on the future. It is (unfortunately) possible both to pray and read the Bible and still have little faith in the future outcome of a given situation. But as we begin to worship, our faith is released and we become more and more "sure of what we hope for and certain of what we do not see."

I want to include here a story of rededication, the purification of the Temple by King Hezekiah.

This might seem to be simply another "example" from the "dedication" category, but there is an extra element in this rededication that is worth noting. This story is found in 2 Chronicles 29:3–36.

When the good King Hezekiah came to power, he began immediately to purify the Temple from the abuses it had endured under King Ahaz. The Levites consecrated themselves and then removed all defilement from the Temple area. On the great day of rededication, many animal sacrifices were made and the Levite singers and instrumentalists were stationed in the Temple. Not only the priests were involved; verse 28 says that the "whole assembly bowed in worship, while the singers sang and the trumpeters played."

The critical part of this passage for us is not the worship itself, but *what happened prior to the worship*. God calls us many times to rededicate ourselves to Him. Before worship and Communion can take place, we must first remove any idols from our lives. These might include anything that has become too high a priority: our careers, our aspirations, our possessions—*anything* that has come between God and us in our hearts.

I once taught a Bible class for young people and remember a discussion we had about the idols mentioned so often in the Bible. One young girl remarked: "I'm glad that I live today and not back then. Thank goodness we don't have any idols in our culture anymore!" How we wish this were true! We might not erect stone statues for the purpose of worship and idolatry, but our culture (perhaps all cultures) is certainly inundated with many idols of different forms.

These idols are not just a distraction from the worship of the Lord, they are a kind of anti-worship. That is why the Bible insists that we be ruthless in their elimination. When they are present, no true worship of God can take place. This is why Augustine wrote of God: "When he is not worshiped *alone,* he is not worshiped."

Corporate Worship in the New Testament

The references to corporate worship in the New Testament are even more diverse than those in the Old. One might say that they begin and end in heaven. That is, the first scene of corporate worship we encounter is the gospel story of the angels in the sky above Bethlehem (see Luke 2:13–14), and the final scene of corporate worship is in heaven as described by the book of Revelation.

Most New Testament books are not historical narratives but letters full of teaching and exhortation. The "examples" that do occur are found in the gospels and the books of Acts and Revelation. They can be classed in six categories: worship toward Jesus, worship of the risen Christ, worship specifically associated with the Holy Spirit, the disciples' praise, worship as a witness and heavenly worship. Let us consider a passage from each category, again with the question in mind, "What is in this passage that we can learn from and apply toward our worship of God?"

Worship Toward Jesus

During Christ's public ministry He was worshiped openly by groups of believers. These times were often associated with major events in His life, such as when the Magi "bowed down and worshiped him" (Matthew 2:11), or when the crowds at the triumphant entry into Jerusalem shouted, "'Hosanna to the Son of David!' 'Blessed is he who comes in the name of the Lord!' 'Hosanna in the highest!'" (Matthew 21:9; see also Mark 11:1–11; Luke 19:28–40; John 12:12–15).

Let us select the scene following His walking on the water of Galilee for our study: "Then those who were in the boat worshiped him, saying, 'Truly you are the Son of God'" (Matthew 14:33). These were not new disciples who had recently met Jesus. They had lived with Him for many months. Yet in this scene the disciples' eyes were fully opened to the reality of Jesus' divinity. They finally saw Him, not just as the Son of Man, but as the Son of God. The realization was overwhelming, and they worshiped Him in awe.

This is the same awe we must have in the presence of Jesus. Even Napoleon, whose conquests made him so majestic in the eyes of those around him, felt awe at the very name of Jesus. He professed: "If Socrates would enter the room we should rise and do him honor. But if Jesus Christ came into the room we should fall on our knees and worship him."

Similarly, if we are to worship God, then we must worship His Son, Jesus. John's first letter is explicit about this: "No one who denies the Son has the Father; whoever acknowledges the Son has the Father also" (1 John 2:23). And Jesus Himself said,

"The Father judges no one, but has entrusted all judgment to the Son, that all may honor the Son just as they honor the Father. He who does not honor the Son does not honor the Father, who sent him" (John 5:22–23).

Specifically, we need to worship Jesus as He truly is—the Savior of the world, our only way to God; not simply a good, moral teacher, but God come in the flesh:

> For by him all things were created: things in heaven and on earth, visible and invisible, whether thrones or powers or rulers or authorities; all things were created by him and for him. He is before all things, and in him all things hold together. And he is the head of the body, the church; he is the beginning and the firstborn from among the dead, so that in everything he might have the supremacy.
>
> Colossians 1:16–18

Worship of the Risen Christ

After the Resurrection, the risen Christ seemed to kindle an ever-deeper response of worship. This is typified by the women who first saw Him: "They came to him, clasped his feet and worshiped him" (Matthew 28:9). This is further attested to by the reaction of Jesus' disciples as they witnessed His ascension into heaven: "They worshiped him and returned to Jerusalem with great joy" (Luke 24:52).

This may seem similar to the lesson we just examined, but there is an important "extra" as we encounter the risen Christ. The key word is *victorious*. The disciples had known that Jesus was very powerful; they saw Him perform many amazing miracles with great authority. Then came the Crucifixion. Had Jesus stayed buried it would have all been over. The disciples' dreams would have been a disappointing memory: Jesus would have shown Himself powerful, but not powerful enough to conquer all.

Then came the Resurrection, proving beyond all doubt that Jesus is victorious over all things. This includes all of our problems, worries and fears. When we worship, we must worship the victorious Jesus who has power over all things and is altogether worthy of our praise. We need to picture the overwhelming joy of the triumphant heavenlies, as Milton described in *Paradise Regained:* "And all heaven admiring stood a space, then into hymns burst forth, and in celestial measures moved, circling the throne and singing, while the hand sung with the voice, and this the argument—'Victory and triumph to the Son of God!'"

As we approach a time of worship, we should ask the Lord to fill us with a greater and greater understanding of who Jesus is— the victorious, risen Christ who has conquered sin and death and sits in eternal triumph at the right hand of God the Father.

Worship Associated with the Holy Spirit

The Acts of the Apostles contains a number of scenes of corporate worship. The first chapter presents a prayer meeting (see verse 14) that could certainly fall under the category of "worship service." In the next chapter we find the great day of Pentecost— note that "they were all together in one place" (2:1)—when the Holy Spirit descended on the apostles: "All of them were filled with the Holy Spirit and began to speak in other tongues as the Spirit enabled them" (verse 4). Verse 11 tells us what they were saying: They were "declaring the wonders of God." The scene is soon complemented by another time of worship and prayer in which "the place where they were meeting was shaken. And they were all filled with the Holy Spirit and spoke the word of God boldly" (Acts 4:31).

Another extraordinary passage is found in the tenth chapter. After Peter spoke to Cornelius and the other Gentiles gathered at his house, an unexpected worship service was initiated (10:44). To the amazement of the Jewish believers present, the Holy Spirit came upon the Gentiles in the home, who began "speaking in tongues and praising God" (verse 46). Perhaps these Jewish believers thought they had God completely figured out, until that surprise visit by the Holy Spirit came their way.

And the questions have not stopped. Most any discussion of the Holy Spirit leads to the debate of whether or not the spiritual gifts are present for the Church today. It is interesting that these verses from Acts are quoted by both charismatics and non-charismatics to prove their points about the work of the Holy Spirit. I will reserve that discussion for chapter 8. Whichever side of that interminable argument you are on, however, I believe that we can all gain many important insights from these passages.

I stated above that we need to pray for a clearer picture of who Jesus is. Perhaps even more so, we need a deeper understanding of Who (not *what!*) the Holy Spirit is. The Holy Spirit is not a thing; He is a person. He may not have a convenient first name like Jesus (when I was a child I actually thought that Jesus' last name was "Christ"), but the Holy Spirit is just as much a *Person* in the Trinity. As with the Father and the Son, we must cultivate a deep relationship with Him through worship.

In the late fourth century, Gregory of Nyssa wrote a letter of correction to those who erred in thought on this subject, in which he conclusively described the person of the Holy Spirit:

> The Holy Spirit is not called the Father or the Son, but all other names by which the Father and the Son are named are applied by scripture to the Holy Spirit also. By this, then we understand the Holy Spirit is above creation. Thus, where the Father and the Son are understood to be, the Holy Spirit is also understood to be.

Jesus said that "you will receive power when the Holy Spirit comes on you" (Acts 1:8). Among other things, one of the principal functions of the Holy Spirit is that of *empowering*. He empowers us to witness (see Acts 1:8), to remember Christ's words (see John 14:26), to discern truth (John 16:13)—to do many righteous acts as a believer. If we are going to worship God in the ways advocated throughout the Scriptures, then we are going to need the empowering of the Holy Spirit.

The Disciples' Praise

A lifestyle of praise is indicative of the disciples' action in the early church. In the last verse of his gospel, Luke recorded that the disciples "stayed continually at the temple, praising God" (Luke 24:53). He then linked this with his second book, for at the end of the second chapter of Acts, we find that the disciples met in the Temple courts every day for fellowship and worship. Furthermore, "they broke bread in their homes," (verse 46) and spent time "praising God" (verse 47).

Since these passages use such expressions as "every day" and "continually," we may safely conclude that these verses represent the activities of many days, months or years. The two verses cited above exemplify the lifestyle of the early Church, one in which worship was a daily practice by all the disciples.

This parallels the Old Testament concept of feasts, as we have already seen. Since "Christ is the end of the law" (Romans 10:4), the Christian Church discontinued many observances of the Old Testament (Passover, Tabernacles, etc.), in favor of a lifestyle of continual worship. This is why Paul wrote the Colossians, "Do not let anyone judge you by what you eat or drink, or with regard to a religious festival, a New Moon celebration or a Sabbath day. These are a shadow of the things that were to come; the reality, however, is found in Christ" (Colossians 2:16–17).

Was Paul advocating that we should worship less than the Old Testament believers? No, he was beseeching that we worship *more!* The lesson for us in the above passages is in the word *continual.* If we are to be known as Christ's disciples, then our worship must be a way of life, not a way of occasional ritual.

Worship as a Witness

One of the smallest but best-known times of New Testament corporate worship is found in chapter sixteen of Acts. I say "smallest" because it involved a congregation of two, Paul and Silas, and the "service" was held at midnight in a prison. Acts 16:25

says that "Paul and Silas were praying and singing hymns to God, and the other prisoners were listening to them." It must have been a very effective service, for the rest of the chapter includes an earthquake, the prisoners' chains coming loose, and the jailer and his family coming to Christ and being baptized.

There is an interesting parallel passage in John Bunyan's celebrated book, *Pilgrim's Progress*.

The two companions, Christian and Hopeful, were thrown into prison by the terrible giant of Doubting Castle. "On Saturday, about midnight, they began to pray, and continued in prayer 'til almost the break of day." Right after this impromptu worship service, Christian realized that he had "a key in my bosom, called Promise, that will, I am persuaded, open any door in Doubting Castle." Sure enough, they were soon out of the prison and safely on the King's Highway.

Because we believe that worship can open spiritual "doors," the midnight worship service from the book of Acts is used as an example of "worship evangelism." Unfortunately, it is also misunderstood. Some people teach from this passage that if we want to evangelize, all we have to do is worship God. This misses the point that the key to Paul and Silas's effective evangelism is that they were worshiping God in the worst of situations. What doubtless impressed their listeners was not simply that these two Christians were worshiping, but that they were worshiping with joy in a situation that would have oppressed and discouraged most people.

Often we make another error concerning our witness before unbelievers or "semi-believers": We assume that we must never make any mistakes around them, that such mistakes will "ruin our witness." But unbelievers are very interested to see how we will react when trouble does come our way. Will we rant and rave in the same way that an unbeliever might? If so, then they will assume (correctly, I am afraid) that all this talk we have about the Christian life is hypocritical nonsense.

Therefore, our best witness is joyful, confident praise when we find ourselves in a crisis. We have already seen in the story

81

about King Jehoshaphat that praise is a powerful weapon of spiritual warfare. It is also clear that if we can react under stress and trials with a spirit of praise, it will be a powerful witness to those around us of the authenticity of the Christian life.

Heavenly Worship

I said earlier that worship in the New Testament both begins and ends in the heavens. We are all familiar with the part of the Christmas story when the angel appears to the shepherds of Bethlehem. The angel tells them of the birth of the Christ Child, and then: "Suddenly a great company of the heavenly host appeared with the angel, praising God and saying, 'Glory to God in the highest, and on earth peace to men on whom his favor rests'" (Luke 2:13–14).

Now we turn to the seven heavenly worship scenes from the book of Revelation. The scenes are: the praise of the four living creatures and the 24 elders (Revelation 4:1–11), the praise of the Lamb worthy to break the seals of the heavenly scroll (Revelation 5:6–14), the worship of the great multitude of saints with the angels of heaven (Revelation 7:9–12), the praise in heaven after the sounding of the seventh trumpet (Revelation 11:15–19), the new song of the 144,000 standing on Mount Zion (Revelation 14:1–3), the song of "those who had been victorious" (Revelation 15:2–5), and the final victory song of the great multitude (Revelation 19:1–7).

As a musician I might note that without the words of these great passages—"Worthy is the Lamb," "The kingdom of this world is become the kingdom of our Lord and of his Christ; and he shall reign for ever and ever," "Hallelujah!"—there would be a lot fewer choruses in Handel's *Messiah!*

What can we possibly learn from all these scenes of worship in the heavenly realms? Certainly it is fine for the saints and angels in heaven to praise God—they haven't the mortal stresses on them that we deal with down here on earth! Most of us take the tacit attitude that "it's easy to worship in heaven, but on earth it can often be quite a challenge."

Yet surely these heavenly portraits teach us something about how to live until we join the joyful congregations of Revelation. I believe the lesson is this: If worship is a characteristic of heaven, then when we truly worship God on earth it is as though we were in heaven—a part of heaven has become real to us. When Jesus taught us to pray "Your kingdom come, Your will be done on earth as it is in heaven," He showed us an important principle of Christian living. We are to live in a kingdom-lifestyle, with a heavenly attitude, as we sojourn here on earth. And perhaps the closest we can get to heaven in this life is in worshiping the King of kings and Lord of lords.

Conclusions

Since we will continue in the next chapter to examine a number of Scriptures, perhaps it is too early to make conclusions. Nevertheless, we end this chapter by reviewing a few of the words that opened it: When we compare corporate worship with private worship, we find that for each worshiper in a corporate meeting, nothing happens internally that could not happen in the privacy of his own home.

Now that we have reviewed biblical "examples" of corporate worship, have we found any evidence to negate this idea? I do not believe so. Do any of the principal insights we have discovered seem to negate it? On the contrary. Taken either individually or as a whole, they strengthen it. As yet, then, we have found no biblical justification for the church's overemphasis on corporate worship at the expense of an individual's private time of worship.

In the next chapter, we will try the opposite approach, focusing on the many scriptural passages concerning private worship. Both the Old and the New Testaments offer us a wide variety of thought-provoking examples.

chapter four

Private Worship in the Bible

I will extol the LORD at all times; his praise will always be on my lips.

Psalm 34:1

Sing to God, not with the voice, but with the heart.

Jerome (A.D. 347–420)

In the last chapter we looked at corporate worship experiences recorded in the Bible. As we turn to Scriptures featuring private worship—that is, worship between one character and God—we will again look for insights to help us in our own times of worship. Some diverse biblical portraits of private worship will help us define what worship is—and what it is not.

By the end of the chapter, we should be thoroughly convinced of the biblical basis for private worship. Indeed, there are far more "examples" of private worship in the Scriptures than of corporate worship.

Private Worship in the Old Testament

The following selections from the Old Testament have been chosen for their diversity. It is as if God were illustrating the lesson that we can worship the Lord in any situation. The circumstances that surround the biblical heroes—Job, Abram, Joshua, Moses, Gideon and David—are very different. Yet each of these situations resulted in private worship.

Worship in Suffering

The book of Job has always given theologians much to ponder and debate. For the purposes of this study, we find in Job an exceptional portrait of integrity and worship. In the opening chapter, Job is told that his sons and daughters have all been destroyed, as well as his riches and property. It is his reaction to this overwhelming news that we will consider.

> At this, Job got up and tore his robe and shaved his head. Then he fell to the ground in worship and said: "Naked I came from my mother's womb, and naked I will depart. The LORD gave and the LORD has taken away; may the name of the LORD be praised." In all this, Job did not sin by charging God with wrongdoing.
>
> Job 1:20–22

Obviously, this passage reveals an incredibly steadfast man for us to emulate, but there is a deeper meaning behind Job's almost superhuman faith. It is not as though he took this terrible news lightly. He tore his robe and shaved his head in the grip of horrendous grief. Yet as agonizing as these events were to him, he was able to worship the Lord. Why?

As we will see more in the next chapter, worship is ultimately based on *relationship*. Job had an enduring relationship with God above all other relationships, even those of his own family. It was for this same reason that King David would one day write, "Though my father and mother forsake me, the LORD will receive me" (Psalm 27:10). The sudden death of Job's dear children could not overrule his even stronger relationship with the Lord. We find, then, a prerequisite to worship: Our relationship with God must be greater than any other relationships we have in this life.

This is the secret of the great martyrs for Christ throughout the centuries. The venerable *Foxes' Book of Martyrs* is filled with the same testimony. For example, when the godly Walter Mill was burned alive for his faith in 1558, his last words were of praise engendered by relationship: "I praise God who hath called me, by his mercy, to seal the truth with my life; which, as I received it from him, so I willingly and joyfully offer it up to his glory." These are the words of a man who knew God intimately and worshiped him constantly.

Worship in Remembrance

Genesis records that Abram, whose name was later changed to Abraham, built four altars (see Genesis 12:7–8; 13:18; 22). The fourth involves the familiar scene in which he bound first his son Isaac and later the ram in his place. The passages concerning the altars read very similarly: "There he built an altar to the LORD and called on the name of the LORD" (Genesis 12:8).

As these altars were built in different parts of Canaan, some commentators believe that they might have been a type of marker to "claim the land" that the Lord had promised to Abram's descendants. Perhaps Abram did have the future in mind for such altars, but a better case can be made that his purpose concerned the past. His first altar came about in this way: "The LORD appeared to Abram and said, 'To your offspring I will give this land.' So he built on altar there to the LORD, who had appeared to him" (Genesis 12:7, emphasis added).

The implication is that he "called on the name of the Lord" out of a devoted heart. Being grateful for such divine meetings, he built the altars *as a remembrance,* a memorial to the meaningful events. As he moved about the land of Canaan, Abram remembered both the Lord's appearance to him and His great promises. As his heart began to overflow with worship, he would build another altar for the Lord.

Like Abraham we, too, need remembrances so that we can look back on "God's track record" to sustain our faith, especially in times of discouragement. Consider the psalmist who began by expressing his cares and doubts:

> "Has God forgotten to be merciful? Has he in anger withheld his compassion?" Then I thought, "To this will I appeal: the years of the right hand of the Most High." I will remember the deeds of the LORD; yes, I will remember your miracles of long ago.
>
> Psalm 77:9–11

In times of trial, when worshiping God seems impossible, we need to remember His past kindness to us. Perhaps our altars might take the shape of written journals, photographs or other memorials of our past walk with the Lord. We can always remember how God has "appeared to us" in the past and worship Him in faith that He will never leave us or forsake us.

Worship and Divine Guidance

Everyone knows the famous story of how the walls of Jericho came crashing down. Immediately before this event, the Bible relates a short but significant scene:

Now when Joshua was near Jericho, he looked up and saw a man standing in front of him with a drawn sword in his hand. Joshua went up to him and asked, "Are you for us or for our enemies?" "Neither," he replied, "but as commander of the army of the LORD I have now come." Then Joshua fell facedown to the ground in reverence, and asked him, "What message does my Lord have for his servant?" The commander of the LORD's army replied, "Take off your sandals, for the place where you are standing is holy." And Joshua did so.

Joshua 5:13–15

Who was this "commander of the Lord's army"? Was it an angel? Was it Jesus? Commentators disagree as to his exact identity, but Joshua's reaction seems to indicate that this was the Lord Himself. Why else would the acknowledged leader of Israel fall "facedown to the ground in reverence"? Some translations say "in worship." Joshua would not have done so for any national leader. He would only have such a worshipful response to the Lord.

We should highlight not only the actual worship but the submissive question Joshua asked while facedown in reverence: "What message does my Lord have for his servant?" In other words, "What would You have me do?" Not only is Joshua worshiping his Lord, he is ready to do anything that God should ask of him. He has completely opened himself to the Lord's divine guidance.

So it is with us. Worship and divine guidance should go hand in hand. When we are truly worshiping the Lord, we are open to whatever way God should desire to lead us. An engaging picture is given in Psalm 32 in which David speaks to God in loving worship: "You are my hiding place; you will protect me from trouble and surround me with songs of deliverance" (verse 7). In reply God promises divine guidance: "I will instruct you and teach you in the way you should go; I will counsel you and watch over you" (verse 8). Worship opens our ears to hear the guidance we need from the Lord.

89

Worship and Intercession

Exodus 34 gives us the inspiring story of God's instructions to Moses to cut new stone tablets to replace the two that were broken. Moses did so, ascending Mount Sinai, where "the LORD came down in the cloud and stood there with him and proclaimed his name, the LORD" (Exodus 34:5). At this meeting, "Moses bowed to the ground at once and worshiped" (Exodus 34:8).

In the very next verse, Moses began to intercede with God for His people: "'O Lord, if I have found favor in your eyes,' he said, 'then let the Lord go with us. Although this is a stiff-necked people, forgive our wickedness and our sin, and take us as your inheritance'" (Exodus 34:9). The Lord assented to this plea and gave a number of specific commands concerning His covenant.

There was no "break" between Moses' humble worship and his intercession. This is because of a principle converse to the one concerning divine guidance. Just as worship opens the door for the Lord to speak to us for guidance, worship also opens a clear channel for us to speak to God in intercession.

Rather than "barging into the throne room" with all our requests and entreaties, we should begin our prayer time with worship. We should first recognize to Whom we are addressing our petitions by worshiping Him as our King, our Father, our Redeemer. In this way our relationship has been renewed and we approach Him as a true suppliant with our intercessions. This is the way the apostle Paul—*before* his great prayer in Ephesians 3:16–21, one of the most powerful prayers in the entire Bible—prefaced his words: "For this reason I kneel before the Father" (Ephesians 3:14).

Worship in Gratitude

The Lord assigned Gideon a tremendous task: to defeat the powerful Midianite army. He was further challenged to reduce his own army to only three hundred men. God knew that Gideon would need encouragement so during that night the LORD said to Gideon, "Get up, go down against the camp, because I am going to give it into your hands. If you are afraid to attack, go down to the camp with your servant Purah and listen to what they are saying. Afterward, you will be encouraged to attack the camp."

Judges 7:9–11

Gideon obeyed as instructed. He arrived secretly at the enemy's massive camp just in time to hear one soldier tell another of a dream about a loaf of bread tumbling into their camp and destroying it. Imagine Gideon's feeling when he overheard the second soldier's startling interpretation: "This can be nothing other than the sword of Gideon son of Joash, the Israelite. God has given the Midianites and the whole camp into his hands" (Judges 7:14). The following verse says it all: "When Gideon heard the dream and its interpretation, *he worshiped God*" (verse 15, emphasis added). And of course, he attacked that night with amazing success.

Why did God allow Gideon to hear about this enemy's dream and its interpretation? Certainly to encourage him in his difficult task, but is that all? The Lord loves to deepen our relationship with Him, and we have already seen this is done through our worship. God knew that Gideon would respond to this encouragement with a heart of gratitude. Often the Lord will give us encouragement—not only to comfort and inspire us but also to draw us closer to Him in worship.

In the previous chapter we saw that worship should be our immediate response when something unexpectedly wonderful comes our way. What about the dozens of little encouragements that happen almost without our notice—the highway you chose was the only one moving, the left-on oven did not burn down your house, the meeting to which you were late had not started yet—can we not worship God for these blessings as well? C. S. Lewis reminds us that "*All* is gift"—that is, everything we have is from God. We need to train ourselves to remember that every single blessing is sent not only to keep us going but also to evoke grateful worship to the Lord.

Worship and God's Answers to Our Prayers

Proverbs 3:6 commands us "in all our ways [to] acknowledge him," but this is easier some times than others. We often ask God for something and in His infinite wisdom He answers us in the negative. This was true for King David as well when his infant son was deathly ill. "David pleaded with God for the child. He fasted and went into his house and spent the nights lying on the ground" (2 Samuel 12:16). This persisted seven days, and then the child died.

Those around David were afraid to tell him the grievous news. Yet when he was told of his son's death, David was able to acknowledge the Lord with admirable resignation: "Then David got up from the ground. After he had washed, put on lotions and changed his clothes, he went into the house of the LORD and worshiped" (2 Samuel 12:20).

This reaction astonished his counselors, for they expected the king to react in desperation. David, however, had prepared his heart to accept either answer, yes or no, from the Lord. It is as though he had already decided in his heart to worship God regardless of the actual outcome of his prayers.

It is tempting to "make deals" with the Almighty. We often say, in effect, "God, if You will answer my prayer this time, I will then worship You." Is it right to hold God hostage until He gives us the answer we desire? Obviously not. This does not mean we should not persevere in prayer. That is certainly our duty. But when we ask God for something, we must first determine in our hearts to worship Him whether He chooses to answer in the positive or the negative.

Private Worship in the New Testament

If there is one writer of New Testament books who is especially enthusiastic about the subject of worship, it is Luke. Though he tells us essentially nothing directly about himself, he must have been a passionate worshiper. So many scenes of worship are found in Luke's gospel and the Acts of the Apostles that, placed together, they might be called the "Psalter" of the New Testament. Let's consider a few of Luke's portraits, as well as those of other books.

The Worship of Joy

After Mary humbly accepted the role of mother to the Messiah, she visited the home of Zechariah and Elizabeth—who was pregnant with John (who would one day be called "The Baptist"). Elizabeth told Mary: "As soon as the sound of your greeting reached my ears, the baby in my womb leaped for joy" (Luke 1:44). (Incidentally, this joyful worship *in utero* gives John the Baptist the record for being the youngest known person to worship the Lord.) It is Mary's response that is of particular interest to us.

The mother of Jesus overflowed with praise: "My soul doth magnify the Lord" (Luke 1:46, rendered here in the poetic King James Version).

The following text (often called the "Magnificat," from the first word in the Latin translation) has been set to breathtaking music throughout the centuries by dozens of master composers. The essence of Mary's grateful praise is found in verse 49: "For the Mighty One has done great things for me—holy is his name." It must have been difficult for Bible translators to refrain from placing exclamation marks after each of her sentences.

If one ponders Mary's situation at that moment, one finds that her life is filled with the starkest of contrasts. On one hand, she was an unwed mother (in a not-too-understanding society), she was poor, and she may have felt nauseous—especially after her long and uncomfortable travel. On the other hand, she knew that she had been chosen by the Lord to carry within her the Savior of the world—God Himself come to earth—and that she would become renowned throughout human history: "From now on all generations will call me blessed" (Luke 1:48).

Aware of these two contradictions, Mary must have made a conscious choice to see her situation in the latter positive light and to ignore the negative. This ongoing decision filled her heart with unspeakable joy, which was prepared to overflow at any given stimulus—as this passage clearly demonstrates.

This also gives us one of the finest examples to emulate in all of Scripture. Can we also refuse to allow our unfavorable circumstances to drag us down? The great Russian writer Leo Tolstoy once remarked: "Happiness does not depend on outward things, but on the way we see them." When we choose to see the negatives around us as the temporary distractions that they really are and to be grateful for the Lord's true blessings in our lives, praise and worship will overflow in our hearts as well.

When we are feeling overwhelmed by anxiety, trouble or stress, we need to praise God to break out of this negative trap. Sometimes this is painfully difficult, unless one reexamines the positives in one's life as Mary must have. In such agonizing times you might ask yourself such questions as: Am I in good health? Do I have friends? Do I have any family members who care for me? Have I had a good education that might prepare me to remedy such troubles as these? Even in our blackest moments, as we choose to appreciate the many positives of our lives we can begin to praise God. Then worship can flow from us as we sing our own "magnificat." For each of us can truthfully say, "The Mighty One has done great things for me."

Praise from Repentance

This same first chapter of Luke highlights another life, that of Zechariah, whose story also ends with joyful praise—but only after a tenuous start. Unlike Mary, who had received her angelic visit with faith, Zechariah expressed doubts when confronted with the words of the angel Gabriel. This messenger from God was not someone to tangle with:

> The angel answered, "I am Gabriel. I stand in the presence of God, and I have been sent to speak to you and to tell you this good news. And now you will be silent and not able to speak until

the day this happens, because you did not believe my words, which will come true at their proper time."

Luke 1:19–20

Sure enough, Zechariah was immediately struck dumb. Later, his wife, Elizabeth, became pregnant as the angel had said, yet Zechariah still could not speak. Only after the birth and the father's insistence at naming the child "John" (as had been commanded by Gabriel) was he set free. "Immediately his mouth was opened and his tongue was loosed, and he began to speak, praising God" (Luke 1:64). He burst into a song of prophetic worship, giving praise to God and speaking of the future mission of his young son (see Luke 1:67–79).

To go nine months or so without speaking was quite an annoying retribution. (As most pregnant women tend to desire a quiet environment, we may assume that this punishment did not bother Elizabeth as much.) Imposed silence often results in more than the usual amount of contemplation. What was Zechariah thinking all those months? Since it was already clear that his doubts had been foolish and unwarranted, he must have chastised himself many times for doubting an angel of God. In short, he was surely in a time of deep repentance.

These indispensable times of personal, soul-cleansing repentance cannot help but be followed by exhilarated worship: We rejoice that our relationship with the Lord, which had been hindered, is restored. This is most evident in the paramount experience of repentance: when a new believer enters the Kingdom of God. "There is rejoicing in the presence of the angels of God over one sinner who repents" (Luke 15:10). In fact, praise is a natural outcome any time that we are convicted of sin and determine to renounce and turn away from it and turn back to the Lord.

Peace Within Worship

Another fascinating character who appears exclusively in Luke's gospel is Simeon. Before the eyes of men he was proba-

95

bly a "nobody," but before God this man had quite an extensive résumé:

> Now there was a man in Jerusalem called Simeon, who was right-eous and devout. He was waiting for the consolation of Israel, and the Holy Spirit was upon him. It had been revealed to him by the Holy Spirit that he would not die before he had seen the Lord's Christ.
>
> Luke 2:25–26

We have all heard the Christmas story so often that the astonishing wonder of this last sentence is usually lost on us. The Jews had been waiting *centuries* for the Christ to appear; if Simeon made this amazing claim openly he may have been thought a madman.

Nevertheless, Simeon had discerned the Holy Spirit's promise correctly. He knew that he could not die until he had fulfilled his destiny of meeting the Messiah, and he was restless in his spirit longing for the day. It reminds us of Augustine's famous phrase from the *Confessions:* "Thou hast made us for thyself, and restless is our heart until it comes to rest in Thee."

When the infant Jesus was brought to the Temple, Simeon, "moved by the Spirit, . . . went into the temple courts" and met the family. Luke records that Simeon took the baby in his arms

> and praised God, saying: "Sovereign Lord, as you have prom-ised, you now dismiss your servant in peace. For my eyes have seen your salvation, which you have prepared in the sight of all people, a light for revelation to the Gentiles and for glory to your people Israel."
>
> Luke 2:28–32

As we picture this scene in our minds, our eyes are drawn to this old man of praise. His expression was doubtless one of seren-ity, his great hope having now been fulfilled, and his heart full of peace and blissful resignation. Here is a man who truly imbibed of "the peace of God, which transcends all understanding" (Philippians 4:7). One can imagine that the rest of his days were spent in peaceful gratitude, worshiping daily as he looked forward to being home with his Lord.

This "peace of God" and worship have an interesting relationship. As we have already seen, it is not necessary to have this peace before worshiping the Lord, but true worship always produces this peace. As we begin to praise God, focusing our hearts and our thoughts upon Him, the cares of this world fall away and we are left with His peace—a peace such as the world cannot give (see John 14:27).

Worship with Eyes Wide Open

An entire chapter of John's gospel is devoted to the story of an unnamed man, an impoverished beggar born blind. Jesus healed him on a Sabbath, which gave the Pharisees yet another opportunity of proving their ineptitude.

They investigated thoroughly, calling in the man who was healed, then his parents, then the man again, and finally throwing him out of fellowship. It is the end of the story on which we will focus.

Jesus found him again, and asked him,

> "Do you believe in the Son of Man?"
>
> "Who is he, sir?" the man asked. "Tell me so that I may believe in him." [Jesus surely must have smiled at the subtle pun he was about to say to a formerly blind man.]
>
> Jesus said, "You have now *seen* him; in fact, he is the one speaking with you."
>
> Then the man said, "Lord, I believe," and he worshiped him.
>
> John 9:35–38, emphasis added

This unnamed believer had his eyes opened twice. Once in verse 7, when his physical eyes were healed, and again in verse 38, when his spiritual eyes were opened to the Lord Jesus. Most of us have seen hundreds of scenes (from church, and even movies!) where fellow-believers *close their eyes* to worship the Lord. Perhaps we are used to this custom as well. There is certainly nothing wrong with this and for many of us it helps close off the distractions so we can concentrate on the Lord. Nevertheless, it is not commanded by Scripture and does not make our worship any "holier."

The point is that whether we worship with our physical eyes open or closed, it is imperative that our spiritual eyes be wide open to the Lord. That is, we always must be focused on and aware of the direction of our worship: God and God only. To worship is to open our eyes to an ever-widening portrait of the Almighty, the only one in the universe who is to be worshiped.

Worship Under Persecution

The next scene of private worship that we view from the New Testament gives us the perfect answer to the question: How should you want to end your life? Answer: worshiping the Lord.

In chapter six of Acts, we read that Stephen was chosen to be among the first deacons of the Christian church. In chapter seven, he was chosen to be the Church's first in a long line of martyrs (still happening today in many parts of the world). His last actions were to preach a powerful sermon, worship God and forgive his enemies. For the Christian, this is about as magnificent an ending to a life as one can imagine.

At the end of the sermon, which so angered his accusers in the Sanhedrin, "Stephen, full of the Holy Spirit, looked up to heaven and saw the glory of God, and Jesus standing at the right hand of God" (Acts 7:55). When he proclaimed this aloud, his opponents dragged him out of the city and began the painful process of stoning him to death. Even under this torture, he was worshiping the Lord: "Stephen prayed, 'Lord Jesus, receive my spirit.' Then he fell on his knees and cried out, 'Lord, do not hold this sin against them.' When he had said this, he fell asleep" (Acts 7:59–60).

What a stirring picture of worship under the worst of persecution! How was Stephen able to worship even while being stoned to death? Part of the answer has to do with the fact that Stephen was already a man of steadfast worship. He is described as "a man full of faith and of the Holy Spirit," (Acts 6:5) and "a man full of God's grace and power, [doing] great wonders and miraculous signs among the people" (Acts 6:8). Preparation for worshiping his Lord during his time of trial and pain came from long practice.

You may not be called to martyrdom, but "everyone who wants to live a godly life in Christ Jesus will be persecuted" (2 Timothy 3:12). What should our response be? The greatest reaction to persecution is internal (and sometimes external) worship. This principle has been used throughout the centuries. As early as A.D. 200 Tertullian wrote that the persecutions of Rome actually purified the Church and increased its worship of the Lord: "And when is trust in God more strong, and when is there a greater fear of him, than when persecution breaks out? The church is awestruck."

When you are ridiculed because of your beliefs, offer up praise to God. When you are passed over by the world because of your stance for Christ, take time to worship God for this privilege. Remember what the disciples did after they had been severely flogged? They left "rejoicing because they had been counted worthy of suffering disgrace for the Name" (Acts 5:41). Through such worship we can follow in their footsteps.

Worship and Godly Revelations

In the previous chapter we looked at the extraordinary scenes of heavenly corporate worship given in the book of Revelation. The panorama of these spectacles is vast: thousands of believers giving praise to the King of kings. Indeed, the entire book is one of wonder, a vision of many things beyond this world, the true revelation of Jesus Christ. And how did this glorious book begin? It all started with one man in private worship before the Lord.

John was on the small island of Patmos "because of the word of God and the testimony of Jesus" (Revelation 1:9). That is, he was banished to this island because his Christian activities were contrary to the laws of Rome. He tells us that his adventures begin when "on the Lord's Day I was in the Spirit, and I heard behind me a loud voice like a trumpet" (Revelation 1:10).

I was in the Spirit. What does John mean by this phrase? Was he in a trance? Was this some psychological state he had never achieved until that day? Perhaps, but rather than manufacture some esoteric bewilderment for his words, it is easier to believe that he was simply worshiping the Lord.

John, because of his witness for Christ, had been forcibly left on an island prison. It is doubtful that any other Christians were nearby. Yet he faithfully continued to worship God, and his faithfulness was rewarded by the apocalyptic visions that now form the final book of the New Testament.

Do you desire a greater revelation of the Almighty? It begins with worship. Do you desire to see more of your destiny with Christ? Begin by worshiping the Lord. As we worship, we lay ourselves open to the knowledge of the Lord and revelations from God can unfold before us. But this begins with worship.

Conclusions

As we found in the previous chapter, each of the scenes of private worship we have considered can help us in our worship of the Lord. This is in no way an exhaustive list of the scenes of worship in the Bible. Furthermore, in each passage many more lessons and principles could be extracted. But these represent well the biblical approach to worship and collectively form the standard for our Christian walk.

Since a fundamental premise for this book is that our lives should embrace at least as much private worship of God as corporate worship, I ask for one final time:

Have we found any biblical evidence to suggest that . . .

corporate worship is preferred to private worship?

our primary worship to God should be on Sunday morning at church?

anything is happening internally in corporate worship that does not (or could not) happen in private worship?

the Christian should spend more time in corporate worship than in private worship?

The testimony of Scripture clearly answers no to all of these questions. There is simply no justification (or even explanation) in the Bible for the disproportionate emphasis in the church today of corporate worship over an individual's private time of worship. How did the church get into such a state? That is a long, complex story of centuries of church history, much of which is not very edifying. It is not so important to find how this situation deteriorated as it is to acknowledge the problem and rectify it.

Now it is time to correct this situation, to encourage all Christians to worship the Lord every day of their lives. This is truly an indispensable key for living a victorious Christian life. It is the way we were created to live and any deviation can generate problems. To use a modern analogy, if an automobile is "out of line," one of the tires will get extra stress and wear out too quickly. In the same way, if something in our Christian walk is emphasized to the detriment of other important elements, our life with God is "out of line" and will suffer the consequences.

As we have seen, this disproportionate emphasis on corporate worship is extensive; it is found throughout the world in virtually every Christian denomination. "How," you may ask, "do I propose to rectify such a large and complex situation in the Body of Christ?"

The answer? The only way *any* problem of this scope is ever corrected: one Christian at a time. And this can begin with you, today.

chapter five

The Essence of Worship: Relationship

O LORD, you are my God; I will exalt you and praise your name, for in perfect faithfulness you have done marvelous things, things planned long ago.

Isaiah 25:1

For there is a joy not granted to the wicked but only to those who worship thee thankfully—and this joy thou thyself art. The happy life is this: to rejoice to thee, in thee, and for thee. This is joy and there is no other.

Augustine, Bishop of Hippo

By now I am sure you have noticed that the English word *worship* has several different meanings. Sometimes it refers to any generic church service. At other times it means singing praise, praying, reading Scripture and many other "holy" actions. Before going any further, it is time to consider a few definitions.

The Difference Between "worship" and "Worship"

A good start is a dictionary. Most give the word *worship* in both its noun and verb forms. Furthermore, there are two basic definitions for each—two for the noun form and two for the verb form. Therefore, we find:

Noun form:
1. a prayer meeting, church service or other rite showing reverence for a deity
2. intense love or admiration of any kind

Verb form:
1. to show religious reverence for
2. to have intense love or admiration for

(There are other forms listed, such as the British title of honor used to address magistrates, but for our purposes we will consider those listed above. My apologies to any British magistrates reading this book.)

The two definitions (whether in noun or verb form) apply roughly to the two types of worship we have been considering: corporate worship and private worship. Of course, this is not a perfect fit, but an important parallel exists. The first definition refers to meetings and church services; the second concerns a *relationship* between you and God, Whom you are worshiping.

The English word *worship* comes from the Anglo-Saxon *weorthscipe*, which means "worthy," "worthwhile" or "having worth." The concept is simply that to be worshiped, one must

104

have worth—one must be worthy of being worshiped. I refer once more to Thomas á Kempis' *Imitation of Christ,* which reminds us of this essential concept: "Would that for but one day I could serve you worthily! Truly you are worthy of all service, all honor, and everlasting praise!"

And these words are but an echo of the praise services of heaven: "You are worthy, our Lord and God, to receive glory and honor and power, for you created all things, and by your will they were created and have their being" (Revelation 4:11).

Since the Bible was written primarily in Hebrew and Greek, let us also look at the word *worship* in these languages. Actually, several different words are translated "worship" in the Bible. The two principal ones in the Old Testament are *hishahawah* (meaning "a bowing down") and *abodah* (meaning "service"). The two main Greek words for *worship* in the New Testament are *proskuneo* (meaning "to bow down" or "to kiss the hand") and *lattreuo* (meaning "to render honor or homage"). Each of these reveals aspects of worship as we know it.

As to the question "What actions can worship encompass?" we noted in the first chapter that almost anything can be done "in a spirit of worship." Worship can include not only singing and praying, but also shaving, washing, painting, mopping or jogging.

So, what *is* worship? What does all this tell us? After the two previous chapters of biblical "examples" of corporate and private worship—plus all these definitions to consider—we are approaching data-overload.

Since the primary purpose of this book—as you have doubt-less perceived—is to encourage each of us in *private* worship, a simple solution is proposed. We need a term that will refer specif-ically to *times of private worship, just between you and God, in which you are not praying or interceding or employing any externals, such as reading from a Bible, but simply worshiping God, period.*

From now on in this book, for the sake of clarity, whenever this highest and most absolute form of worship is being referred to it will be capitalized: Worship.

This Worship (notice capitalization) could include many activities you do with others or by yourself, such as playing an instrument, Bible reading and interceding for others. We will use it, however, to refer solely to something you do *alone* with God, focusing on Him without externals—even prayer needs—of any kind.

One might say that this is Worship in its purest form, "like silver refined in a furnace of clay, purified seven times" (Psalm 12:6). It is not the only way God can or should be worshiped but it is the ultimate form for a Christian to aspire to, as it necessitates that there be nothing whatsoever coming between you and the Lord.

In this context, the word *praise* can be used synonymously with Worship. In corporate settings, ministers of music often make a distinction between "praise songs" (usually fast loud songs) and "worship songs" (usually slow reverent songs). In a private setting, both types would be considered Worship songs.

Exhortations from Scripture

If we were to review the historical "examples" of private worship that we focused on in the last chapter, we would find that many of them fit this use of the word *Worship*. From Job to Gideon, from the blind man Jesus healed to John on the island of Patmos, these men exhibited intense love and adoration for God without the use of externals in their private worship.

We have not yet focused on the many "exhortations" about worship found in Scripture. Do they also advocate Worship in this pure sense?

Many do, but not all. The dozens of Scriptures that entreat us to "Praise the Lord!" can be fulfilled in both corporate and private worship, both with and without externals.

Furthermore, when the Bible tells us to "praise God in His sanctuary" or "in the great congregation," we should interpret these as specific commands to worship corporately with brothers and sisters in the Lord. (Please keep in mind that this book is not to discourage corporate worship, which is obviously commanded in the Scriptures. My thesis is that it should not be practiced *exclusively*, with little or no private worship in our lives.)

Still, the Bible is filled with "exhortations" to praise God in the context of private worship. A few such "exhortations" are:

"Worship the LORD your God, and his blessing will be on your food and water. I will take away sickness from among you."

Exodus 23:25

When you have eaten and are satisfied, praise the LORD your God for the good land he has given you.

Deuteronomy 8:10

"The LORD lives! Praise be to my Rock! Exalted be God, the Rock, my Savior!"

2 Samuel 22:47

I will extol the LORD at all times; his praise will always be on my lips.

Psalm 34:1

But I will sing of your strength, in the morning I will sing of your love; for you are my fortress, my refuge in times of trouble.

Psalm 59:16

Then will I ever sing praise to your name and fulfill my vows day after day.

Psalm 61:8

I will praise you as long as I live, and in your name I will lift up my hands. My soul will be satisfied as with the richest of foods; with singing lips my mouth will praise you. On my bed I remember you; I think of you through the watches of the night.

Psalm 63:4–6

My mouth is filled with your praise, declaring your splendor all day long.

Psalm 71:8

It is good to praise the LORD and make music to your name, O Most High, to proclaim your love in the morning and your faithfulness at night.

Psalm 92:1–2

Seven times a day I praise you for your righteous laws.

Psalm 119:164

Every day I will praise you and extol your name for ever and ever.

Psalm 145:2

(Note: There are too many verses in the Psalms on this subject to list here. Some others you might want to check are: 7:17; 16:7; 28:6–7; 30:4; 33:1–3; 42:5; 47:6–7; 86:11–12; 96:9; 99:5; 101:1; 103:1–2; 104:33; 106:1; 112:1; 119:7; 119:108; 119:171; 139:14; 146:1–2; and 147:1.)

O LORD, you are my God; I will exalt you and praise your name.

Isaiah 25:1

Praise be to the God and Father of our Lord Jesus Christ, who has blessed us in the heavenly realms with every spiritual blessing in Christ.

Ephesians 1:3

Is anyone happy? Let him sing songs of praise.

James 5:13

We could list many other verses of similar nature, but these give us a good enough sampling to ask the following questions:

Do these verses give any indication of corporate worship? Do they suggest a gathering of believers, a building or any externals whatsoever?

When the psalmist declares "Seven times a day I praise You," does he have to call his friends together for praise each of the seven times? When he claims that "on my bed I remember you," surely he does not have the congregation together on one mattress under the covers.

These passages, and many others, describe the beauty of pure Worship. There is no congregation, no prayers of petition, no Bible verses to read. The worshiper is simply caught up in a wonderful state of Worship and relationship with his Lord.

"In Spirit and in Truth"

Other biblical passages, which are not single verses but rather extended excerpts, might fit into this category of "exhortations." Such is the case of John 4:19–24, one of the most famous passages in the Bible. It is part of a conversation between Jesus and a Samaritan woman He met at a well. When Jesus revealed that He knew all about her, she began the section that so closely concerns our topic:

> "Sir," the woman said, "I can see that you are a prophet. Our fathers worshiped on this mountain, but you Jews claim that the place where we must worship is in Jerusalem."
>
> Jesus declared, "'Believe me, woman, a time is coming when you will worship the Father neither on this mountain nor in Jerusalem. You Samaritans worship what you do not know; we worship what we do know, for salvation is from the Jews. Yet a time is coming and has now come when the true worshipers will worship the Father in spirit and truth, for they are the kind of worshipers the Father seeks. God is spirit, and his worshipers must worship in spirit and in truth."
>
> John 4:19–24

There are at least as many interpretations of this passage as there are worship leaders today. Furthermore, most of the great Christian writers throughout the centuries—from the early Church Fathers to many contemporary preachers—have discovered an abundance of insights from these verses.

Rather than debate with all the great Christian minds of the ages, I will mention only three points from this passage that concern the topic of this book.

First, location (in Jerusalem, on a mountain, in a church, in a worship service) is not a consequential factor in our worship of God. This key point directly supports the underlying premise of private worship: that we should worship God anywhere and everywhere, not just on certain days (Sunday) in certain places (your church) with certain people (your congregation and worship leader).

Second, the Father is *seeking* (that is, desiring) those who will worship Him in the correct manner. This point is so important as to merit further discussion; see below: "Why Does God Desire Our Worship?"

Third, since God is Spirit, this correct manner is to worship Him in spirit and in truth. It is on this third point that many of the great writers and preachers cannot agree. Some believe that to worship Him "in spirit and in truth" means simply to worship the Triune God. Others believe it indicates that our worship is accepted only if our hearts are pure and full of the truth. Still others insist that it refers to a mystical or charismatic state of worship. There are dozens of ideas about this verse, nearly all of which are quite intriguing.

Whatever you believe that Jesus specifically meant by this phrase *in spirit and in truth*, a point of agreement with all commentaries is that our worship should be more spiritual than natural. That is, our focus should not be on the natural surroundings (location, song books, other worshipers), but rather the spiritual—God Himself.

Why Does God Desire Our Worship?

Let's return to the second point in the short list above. This passage about Jesus and the woman at the well informs us that the Father is seeking (that is, desires) our worship. Perhaps some of you, after pondering this idea, have asked the classic one-word question, Why?

The many Scriptures we have already read make it clear that God commands us to worship Him. But why? Usually our difficulties with this question can be worded in two ways:

1. Is God conceited, so that He wants to be the center of everything?
2. Does an all-powerful God *need* anything from us?

To answer these questions, look at the character of God. To begin with, "God is love" (1 John 4:16). This means that all He does toward us is done in love—that is, all His actions toward us are done for *our* good. His desire for our worship, therefore, cannot be from any motives of conceit or egotism. We must conclude that He wants us to worship Him for our good. So much for the first question.

The second question is a bit trickier. Obviously, an all-powerful God cannot have needs in the same way that we have needs. As the great London preacher, Charles Spurgeon, pointed out, "The Lord says nothing of friends and helpers: he undertakes the work alone, and feels no need of human arms to aid him."

This is also true regarding worship. It is clear that if no person ever worships the Lord, God has not lost anything. Indeed, God was God—without any needs whatsoever—long before He even created us.

Yet we cannot deny that God commands us to worship Him, although this often seems to be the only solution. This is the case, to give one example, with one of our Founding Fathers, Benjamin Franklin—a man of tremendous intellect and practical wisdom.

In his *Articles of Belief and Acts of Religion,* Franklin declared: "I cannot conceive otherwise that He, the Infinite Father, expects and requires no worship or praise from us, but that He is infinitely above it."

How did he come up with such an idea? Very logically . . . almost.

Franklin discerned correctly that God is "Infinite." This led to his summation that God is all-powerful, all-knowing and infinitely beyond needing worship. Also correct.

There is a mistake in this thinking, however, one of omission. Our brilliant patriot followed the line of thinking that the only reason God might command praise from us is that He *needs* us to praise Him, which, of, course, He does not. Franklin did not see that there might be another reason that God commands us to worship Him.

What is this other reason?

The Essence of Worship: Intimate Relationship with God

The answer reveals one of the most profound aspects of the Christian life. The reason that God desires our Worship is because *He desires a personal relationship with each of his children.*

God desires this relationship with us, not because He needs it, but because of His own nature and character. Everything we see in Scripture indicates that it is in God's essential nature to desire relationship with those He has created. Consider the Lord's words as He cries out for our fellowship: "Here I am! I stand at the door and knock. If anyone hears my voice and opens the door, I will come in and eat with him, and he with me" (Revelation 3:20).

Why else did He create us if it were not to have relationship with us? It is because God is love—and love is essentially concerned with giving—that He created us.

This "desire of God" is poetically described toward the beginning of Milton's *Paradise Lost.* According to this epic masterpiece, as soon as Creation was complete God had an "unspeakable desire to see and know all these his wondrous works, but chiefly Man, his chief delight and favour, him for whom all these works so wondrously he ordained."

Indeed, God desires to show His love to *all* people, even those who do not believe in Him: "He causes his sun to rise on the evil and the good, and sends rains on the righteous and the unrighteous" (Matthew 5:45). Nevertheless, our Lord responds particularly to those who have responded to Him. For example, John's gospel tells us that "to all who received him, to those who believed in his name, he gave the right to become children of God" (John 1:12).

And it is this picture of us as "*children* of God" that gives the best clue in our understanding of the importance of private Worship.

Human Relationships as Models for Worship

In the New Testament our relationship to the Lord is portrayed in a number of different ways. Among other "designations" we are called:

- "children of God" (1 John 3:1)
- "the bride of the Lamb" (that is, Christ) (Revelation 21:9)
- "friends" (of Jesus) (John 15:15)
- "God's fellow worker" (1 Thessalonians 3:2)
- "servants" (Luke 17:10)

As Christians, all of these designations are given to us. At different times in our lives, as well as during different activities, certain titles become more appropriate than others. For example, when we are laboring to bring the Gospel message to those around us, we are truly "God's fellow workers." When we are caring for the sick and the needy, we are taking on the role of a "servant."

When we take time to Worship the Lord, the designations we identify most with are "children of God" and "the bride of Christ." There are several reasons for this.

First, these two relationships are the most natural in which to express total love. When a young child nestles in his or her father's arms or when a young couple pledge themselves to each other—that love is shared openly and expressed freely.

This is not to say that love is not felt in other relationships, such as friendship. The distinction might be that love within friendship is seldom expressed openly but, rather, tacitly. As C. S. Lewis pointed out in his marvelous book *The Four Loves,* the natural placement of two friends is side-by-side, whereas parent/child and bride/groom relationships are face-to-face.

It is this face-to-face posture that we assume with God in true Worship. Charles Spurgeon once described His intimate relationship with the Lord in this way: "I looked at God and he looked at me, and we were one forever."

Furthermore, the husband/wife and parent/child relationships are the most permanent of human associations. The coworkers and even friends you have today may not be there in a few years. Yet marriage is (or certainly should be) an unalterable state until death as is the parent/child relation. Even if your son or daughter marries and moves far away, he or she still remains your son or daughter. These relationships remain our best models for Worship of God, since they reflect the utterly permanent relationship we have with Him.

Finally, these two relationships are the most private and therefore best represent the closeness we have in private Worship. Unlike friends or coworkers—who welcome another member to their group—lovers strive to be alone with each other. And parents who love all of their children treasure special times alone with them individually.

Why Is *Private* Worship Desired in Particular?

We begin to see why God desires for us to Worship Him without the distractions and disruptions that can occur in corporate worship. As a loving husband and wife desire to escape the busy responsibilities of life and be alone with each other, so the Lord desires time alone with us. As a child longs to have the undistracted attention of a parent—not just to play with, but to bond with— so we should long for times of uninterrupted Worship of our Lord.

If this concept of spending time alone in Worship—not in praying or Bible reading but simply in Worship—is new to you, then try picturing yourself in one of these images: as a young child in the lap of your dear father, or as a husband (or wife) in the loving embrace of your spouse. Consider the love expressed to you by the following Scriptures:

"This, then, is how you should pray: 'Our Father. . . .'"

Matthew 6:9

"How often I have longed to gather your children together, as a hen gathers her chicks under her wings."

Luke 13:34

You received the Spirit of sonship. And by him we cry, "Abba, Father." The Spirit himself testifies with our spirit that we are God's children."

Romans 8:15–16

You are all sons of God through faith in Christ Jesus, for all of you who were baptized into Christ have clothed yourselves with Christ.

Galatians 3:26–27

How great is the love the Father has lavished on us, that we should be called children of God! And that is what we are!"

1 John 3:1

"For your maker is your husband—the Lord Almighty is his name—the Holy One of Israel is your Redeemer; he is called the God of all the earth."

Isaiah 54:5

As a bridegroom rejoices over his bride, so will your God rejoice over you.

Isaiah 62:5

"I will betroth you to me forever; I will betroth you in righteousness and justice, in love and compassion. I will betroth you in faithfulness, and you will acknowledge the LORD."

Hosea 2:19–20

"The LORD your God is with you, he is mighty to save. He will take great delight in you, he will quiet you with his love, he will rejoice over you with singing."

Zephaniah 3:17

Husbands, love your wives, just as Christ loved the church and gave himself up for her.

Ephesians 5:25

These and many other passages speak of our relationship to God as intimate, loving and personal. They reveal the Creator of the universe as a person—likened to a compassionate parent or an impassioned spouse—who desires to spend time alone with each one He loves. For us, our response is private Worship.

When we truly recognize and embrace this fundamental concept, we are overcome by God Himself. Brother Lawrence, in *The Practice of the Presence of God*, described his revelation in this manner: "I renounced, for the love of him, everything that was not he. And I began to live as if there was none but he and I in the world."

"Wait a moment!" some of you may be saying. "Can't we have this same relationship with God in a corporate setting? After all, lovers and family members have to live in a world with many other people around them. It is not as though they cease to love each other when someone else walks into the room."

Certainly, a parent loves each of his or her children, whether only one is in the room or a whole group of them. In the same way, no two spouses begin to love each other less when someone else joins them. Nevertheless, when this happens there is a subtle change in the dynamic of the relationship. It is no longer "private." Words of endearment or love and commitment seem out of place in a group setting.

Yet such words are the essence of what we say to God during Worship: "I love You, Lord. I praise You with all my heart. You are worthy of praise and honor and glory." Yes, these certainly can and should be confessed to God in corporate worship, but our hearts are more likely to fill to overflowing when we are alone with our loving Father. And even in a Sunday morning corporate setting, these words will find expression more freely from those who habitually Worship God in private throughout the week.

The Midway Point

We have now come to the dividing point of this book. We have concluded the section "Why Worship?" and move into the section called "How to Worship."

This was intentionally modeled after the writings of Paul who grounded the first part of his letters in theological background and arguments and then concluded with practical "how-to" admonishments. (Two examples are Romans 1–11 and 12–16, and Hebrews 1–11 and 12–13.)

In the previous five chapters we have explored the church's overemphasis on corporate worship and seen that our Lord would have us spend more and more time in private Worship. If you have not yet come to this conclusion, I urge you to search the Scriptures, to meditate and to pray about this assertion.

If you are convinced that God desires you to Worship Him every day "in spirit and in truth," then read on as we hone our skills in the greatest art of all: the fine art of Worship.

part 2

How to Worship

chapter six

Overcoming Barriers to Worshiping God

"Be still, and know that I am God; I will be exalted among the nations, I will be exalted in the earth."

Psalm 46:10

Some claim that I have ensnared the people by the melodies of my hymns. I do not deny it!

Ambrose, Bishop of Milan

The first half of this book established that we need to Worship God (in the capital letter sense) each day—not just in our congregations but also in the privacy of our own homes.

As you will remember this is distinct from the important habit of having a daily "quiet time" with the Lord, which should involve prayer and intercession as well as the study of Scripture. This practice, along with much of our church participation, is often called "worship" because it helps bring us closer to God. Our focus, however, is Worship in a higher, purer sense. During our quiet times alone with the Lord—and on other occasions—we need specifically to worship God without the benefit (or distraction) of externals that are usually part of our prayer times.

The remainder of the book concerns the practical how-to aspects of Worship in our lives. Before considering the many facets of effectual Worship, we need first to deal with some of the major obstacles—which can shut down the effort before it begins. No matter how wonderful your automobile might be, it is of no use to you if the starter malfunctions.

All of us encounter obstacles as we try to do what we know we should do: Worship the Lord. Fortunately, none of us has to deal with all of them! God made each of us unique. You may struggle in an area that your neighbor breezes through, and he stumbles at another place that is easy for you.

Here are some descriptions to help you identify and overcome your problem areas.

Different Personality Types

It may surprise you that this is a barrier to Worship, let alone at the top of the list. Yet this is such a difficulty for so many that it needs to be dealt with at the outset.

Most of us read of King David publicly "dancing before the Lord with all his might" or see someone in our congregation ecstatically praising God and we say to ourselves: *That's not me.* It is all too common for sincere Christians to feel a sense of failure due to their lack of overt expression. Does God really want us (command us?) all to worship Him in the same way?

Of course not. Even within the Scriptures we see a wide variety of expression. The spectrum spans from King David's exuberance to the aged Jacob who "worshiped as he leaned on the top of his staff" (Genesis 47:31). Many other biblical examples fall at various places in between these two.

Let's face it. Though some of us are exuberant dancers, others of us prefer to lean quietly on our staffs.

So, is this O.K.? Well, yes and no.

Yes, we are unique individuals. Who made us this way? God did. He doubtless enjoys each of our personalities, which were a gift from Him. As Paul explains, "We have different gifts, according to the grace given us" (Romans 12:6). The Lord loves people who are analytical or emotional. He loves introverts, extroverts and everyone in between.

Furthermore, the Lord wants to be Worshiped by those of every personality type from the exuberant dancers to the staff leaners. This is one reason why the Bible gives us so many different portraits of Worship, from dancing and leaping (Psalm 149:3) to kneeling down before the Lord (Psalm 95:6). It is our job to find those actions that enhance our times of Worship and to avoid any guilt trips about what we are doing (or not doing).

Yes, it is appropriate for you to Worship God in your own "style." The important thing is *to Worship*, not to Worship in a certain way. In fact, any fixation on our personal preferences can become a hindrance to Worship. That is why the answer to the above question "Is this O.K.?" is sometimes no.

No, we must never use our personalities as an excuse not to Worship the Lord. If we are naturally withdrawn, reclusive or even crotchety, we still must remind ourselves that God *commands* us all to Worship Him. No excuses.

Those of us who find it difficult to praise the Lord may be comforted in the knowledge that He understands our difficulties. He knows that this is a challenge and is surely all the more pleased with us for our extra efforts. He knows that some of us Worship more easily than others, but this does not diminish the fact that *all* of us need to spend time Worshiping our Creator.

Granted, it is hard sometimes to determine where our natural personalities end and an area of sin begins. For instance, it is not a sin to be a reserved person, but it becomes so if it leads to inhospitality toward others in need. It is fine to be gregarious and enjoy society, but there are many Scriptures about "controlling the tongue." The Bible commends a "gentle and quiet spirit," but not if this becomes an excuse never to witness verbally for Christ.

We need to take an honest look at our natural personalities and find our distinctive ways of Worshiping God. By the same token we must never use our personality types as excuses for ingratitude or a lack of Worship.

If it seems difficult or unnatural to praise God, discipline yourself to do so anyway. God will give you the grace needed, and the more you Worship God, the easier and more natural it will become. Like any other action we do in life, from playing the piano to driving a car, the act of Worship is improved with practice.

Our Upbringings and Other Painful Memories

In the previous chapter, we saw how the Lord helps us in our ability to Worship by giving us models of natural relationships—which are analogous to the ultimate relationship we have with God. We saw how the Bible calls us "children of God" and the "bride of Christ."

Picturing ourselves in one of these images—as a young child in the lap of your dear father or a wife or husband in the loving embrace of your spouse—is much more difficult for some of us than others.

It is not very pleasurable to imagine yourself in the loving embrace of a spouse, if your husband (who incessantly beat you) just deserted you to marry your best friend. It is equally painful to contemplate being in the lap of your dear father, if the only father you ever knew was cold, abusive or virtually absent. This area of painful memories reveals one of the most problematic barriers to Worship. One does not have to be an experienced psychologist to realize that our ongoing relationships with God are affected by our relationships with our parents, especially our fathers. In the formative years, our pictures of God are subconsciously modeled after the way we see our natural fathers. For many of us, this is not a very comforting picture.

As was mentioned earlier, each of us has to deal with different barriers to Worship, and none of us has to deal with them all. I should interject here that I had the great blessing of having two wonderful, loving and supportive parents. I have further been blessed with a fantastic marriage with a beautiful, godly woman for more than 25 years. By God's grace this is one barrier I have not had much trouble with. (I have other ones.)

Yet I have spent many hours counseling those who have not enjoyed these blessings and have seen the overwhelming pain and insecurity that result from never having a loving father. If you have suffered in this sorrowful component of life, please try to accept more and more what the Scriptures reveal about your heavenly Father.

He is not like the remote, selfish or abusive father with whom you grew up. God is the Ultimate Father. He loves you more than you can comprehend. He is ever-present, ever-encouraging, ever-understanding, ever-comforting. God is love, straight through; He is the opposite of fear. Comparing God to your earthly father (even to the best of earthly fathers) is like comparing a beautiful sunset to a common stone.

King David said with confidence, "Though my father and mother forsake me, the LORD will receive me" (Psalm 27:10). If you feel as though you were neglected by your parents or spouse, remember that God "defends the cause of the fatherless and the widow" (Deuteronomy 10:18). There are many, many Bible promises of this nature, particularly to the *fatherless* (which may be taken either literally or figuratively): "A father to the fatherless, a defender of widows, is God in his holy dwelling" (Psalm 68:5). (See also Exodus 22:22–23; Deuteronomy 14:28–29; Psalm 10:14, 18; 146:9; Proverbs 15:25; 23:10–11; Jeremiah 49:11; Hosea 14:3b; Malachi 3:5; and James 1:27.)

If you are fearful or hesitant of approaching God in Worship because of the painful example of fatherhood you endured or the rejection you suffered from an unfaithful or unloving wife or husband, there is good news for you. You can become a chainbreaker, by God's grace. But it is not easy, and it usually takes time and practice.

Painful memories do not simply go away. We cannot erase the past, but we can change the future. The following illustration may give us our best picture for overcoming such memory barriers:

Suppose you have a glass of pure spring water. Before you can drink it, however, a drop of India ink splashes into it. From this one drop, the entire glass of water turns black. Now would you drink this glass of water? Of course not.

Suppose you also have nearby a large tub filled with pure spring water. You take the glass of contaminated water and pour it into the tub. The result is water with only a tinge of black. Would you now drink the water in the tub? Well, maybe . . . but it is still a little dark.

Now suppose you also happen to have a swimming pool filled with pure spring water. (A lot of supposing is needed for this illustration!) You take the water from the tub and pour it into the pool. There is no perceptible change at all in the huge amount of water. It looks, and even tastes, perfectly fine. Would you drink from this? Undoubtedly.

What has happened to the powerful India ink? It is still there but it has been so utterly diluted as to become harmless. So it is with our painful, negative memories. We cannot make them go away, but we can continue to add more and more and more positive experiences with Christ so as to eventually negate the distorting influence of the bitter remembrances. And spending time

Worshiping your true Father is like pouring gallons of fresh, healing water into our thirsty and wounded souls.

Sin Unrepented

Sin barriers are completely different from barriers of painful memories. A faulty image of God caused by the memory of an abusive father is not something you chose—it was thrust upon you against your will; sin is *your choosing* to do wrong. Memories involve something that occurred in the past, but sin unrepented happens in the living present. And ongoing sinful activities in our lives will form an impenetrable barrier to our Worship of God. As John Bunyan points out in *Pilgrim's Progress,* "One leak will sink a ship; and one sin will destroy a sinner."

As we noted in the previous chapter, to Worship God is to be in the position of "face-to-face." Now consider the first two verses of Isaiah 59: "Surely the arm of the LORD is not too short to save, nor his ear too dull to hear. But your iniquities have separated you from your God; your sins have hidden his face from you, so that he will not hear."

Another significant verse on this subject is Psalm 66:18, where David, in a context of worship, admits: "If I had cherished sin in my heart, the Lord would not have listened." This seems to indicate that when we are in sin, even if we should go through the motions of Worshiping God, it would be a worthless exercise.

We are all, of course, sinners. And we sin every day. But we need to be in a continual state of self-examination and confession, to keep "short accounts" with the Lord. Any known sin areas in our lives must be guarded against and repented of as we pray for God's forgiveness and help. David prayed in Psalm 19:12–13: "Forgive my hidden faults. Keep your servant also from willful sins; may they not rule over me."

Unlike the India ink illustration concerning the healing of painful memories, sin must be ruthlessly rooted out, not covered over. Think of it this way. If I mistakenly type my first name as

"Parick," all I have to do on this word processor to fix the mis-spelling is to insert a *t* between the *a* and the *r* to spell *Patrick*.

But suppose that I mistakenly type my first name as "Pazrick." No amount of adding letters will ever fix the problem. The name cannot be corrected without eliminating the false letter *z*. (In the days of pencil writing, an eraser would be required. I'll just use the backspace key.)

Sin in our life is like that false letter *z*. It must be eradicated, not placated. How? Well, the first step is simply to identify the problem. We must sincerely pray prayers like David's in Psalm 19, imploring God to show us what needs to be changed within us.

You will notice that I do not provide a handy list of sins to pick from. What if you are committing a sin that I forgot to include in such a list? Our sins are as individual as we are. They may be sins of commission or, perhaps more often, sins of omission. One of our ongoing goals in life is to identify and then abdicate them. We would be wise to remember this quote from Thomas Carlyle: "The greatest security against sin is to be shocked by its presence."

When sin becomes known to us, one of the best means of renouncing it is through prayerful accountability. Find someone trustworthy and tell him or her of your desire to be free from the sin area in your life that God has revealed. Ask this person to hold you lovingly accountable and give him or her the delicate freedom to ask you how you are doing in that area until endur-ing victory is achieved.

If the concept of confession and accountability seems drastic to you, good. We need to deal with our sins drastically so that we can Worship the Lord without hindrance. Consider the com-mand of James 5:16: "Therefore confess your sins to each other and pray for each other so that you may be healed." Obviously, the person you choose to hold you accountable must be carefully selected with fervent prayer. But the resulting freedom you will gain through this sometimes painful process of accountability will be worth more than you can imagine.

Time-Pressured Lifestyles

Welcome to the twenty-first century, where it seems as if we are supposed to be twice as busy as we were in the twentieth century. It is a dreadful but revealing sign of the times that when you ask someone "How are you?" the inevitable answer is "Keeping busy!"—as if "busyness" were a virtue in itself. It is not. Diligence and hard work are virtues, but keeping constantly busy is a heinous sin that must be resisted to our dying day.

In the first chapter, we saw that *the spending of our time* is the ultimate stewardship. Time is the great leveler: We are all given the same amount each day. You are given just as many hours, minutes and seconds today as the president of the United States or the CEOs of the largest corporations. It is how you spend this precious time that demonstrates to the world, and to God, what is truly important to you.

This is not an option for Christ's followers. We must find time where we can put the world and all its cares behind and focus everything on Worshiping God. As Edward M. Bounds admonishes us in his book *Power Through Prayer:* "Seek a suitable time for leisure and meditate often on the favors of God. Leave curiosities alone." This immensely important advice, which should be the keystone over the Christian lifestyle, takes a degree of discipline for all of us.

How many times have I been told: "I want to spent time with the Lord, but I just can't find the time"? To which I respond (I hope with a degree of compassion!): "Then one can only conclude that God must not be very important to you." The person then raves: "No, no! He is very important to me. I just can't find time for Him." And so it goes.

There are two kinds of people who say such things. One is the lackluster Christian who has confessed Christ as Savior and maybe tries to get to church when he can—in the midst of a thousand other activities. There is not much that we can do for spiritual mediocrity, except to pray for the person to get serious with God and to encourage him in this as he gives us opportunity.

But it is a different story for the second type of Christian who says (and really means it): "God is very important to me. I just can't find time for Him." If this person is sincere, he or she can find the time for Worshiping God. This person simply needs help in taking control of his or her time.

Sometimes a Christian will object to this idea, and insist, "I don't want to be in the driver's seat of my life. God is in the driver's seat." The sentiment is right but the application is befuddled. God owns everything, but when He gives you stewardship over something, He expects you to take control.

God "owned" the Garden of Eden. He did not give Adam and Eve a deed to it. But He put them there "to work it and take care of it" (Genesis 2:15). For that matter, "the earth is the LORD's" (Psalm 24:1), but if you are a farmer you must care for your fields or they will not bear fruit. This is God's way of giving us creative stewardship and responsibility. So it is with our time.

So to those who "can't find the time" for Worshiping God, I say, "Yes you can. You have to *plan*. And you have to pay the price."

Plan beforehand. Determine that every day you will Worship God at _____ o'clock. Then pay the price. Since we all have exactly 24 hours each day, and cannot add anything to it without subtracting something from it, the price is in the subtraction. Perhaps you may have to subtract some TV or sleep or other activity that is of less importance than Worshiping God, but you can find the time, and all of us *must* do so.

The key is to take control of your time *before* letting everything else in the world take control of you. This is a very practical application of the old adage to "put God first." This is also why the Old Testament speaks so often of "firstfruits," and why Jesus commanded us to "seek first his kingdom and his righteousness" (Matthew 6:33).

Focus

This is yet another area in which our twenty-first-century pace works against us. Most of us have been raised on fast food, quick solutions and sound bites. Western society continues to accelerate our daily tempo every year. It seems as though each week I see another article or news story about our children's "attention deficit disorder" and their inability to concentrate for any amount of time.

But it is not just the children, is it? All of us have been infected to some degree by this subtle malady. We abhor waiting in line, being put on hold, even waiting for our computers to warm up. (Those machines were invented, we were told, to save time!)

This affects nearly all of our society. Preachers are now advised to give much shorter sermons than they gave a century ago. Many companies use overnight delivery as a policy, whether quick turnaround is needed or not. In the music world to which I belong, symphonic concerts are cut shorter and shorter. (In Beethoven's day they could last four to six hours.) We seem to have lost the ability to enjoy even the greatest pleasures at any length!

But this is really not a new problem. When Thomas á Kempis wrote *The Imitation of Christ* in the fifteenth century, he noted: "We are too occupied with our own whims and fancies, too taken up with passing things." This was long before we had cell phones, the Internet and Monday Night Football to distract us. Yet á Kempis said that for those who turned away from such diversions, "they were able to attach themselves to God with all their heart and freely to concentrate their innermost thoughts."

What does this have to do with Worship? Simple. God says: "Be still, and know that I am God" (Psalm 46:10). The Bible says: "The LORD is in his holy temple; let all the earth be silent before him" (Habakkuk 2:20). It also commands: "Be still before the LORD, all mankind, because he has roused himself from his holy dwelling" (Zechariah 2:13).

We are in trouble.

Furthermore, as we have seen repeatedly, *Worship takes time.* You cannot "gaze upon the beauty of the LORD" (Psalm 27:4) while you also gaze at your watch. You cannot "meditate on [His] unfailing love" (Psalm 48:9) while you also meditate on tomorrow's deadlines, the roast in the oven or your desire for a chocolate chip cookie.

We can neither worship God by singing at church or reading the Bible nor Worship the Lord by basking in His divine presence unless we have a degree of focus, patience and what might be called "holy concentration."

If you, like most of us, struggle in this area, do not lose hope. God has given us a number of suggestions to help. Although the Lord would have us Worship Him without the distractions of externals, He has given us many *internal* aids to help us keep our concentration.

These we shall explore fully in the remaining chapters, but here is a quick glimmer. Suppose you are alone with God, Worshiping Him in great love, but losing attention. How about using an internal aid, the most obvious being *speech*, to help you refocus? "With my mouth I will greatly extol the LORD" (Psalm 109:30). We will investigate many other internal aids to Worship, but in the meantime we must recognize that they will all require a degree of discipline and concentration.

The Enemy of Worship

This is listed last, not because it is the least consequential, but because I hate to give the devil any more credit than absolutely necessary. As C. S. Lewis discerned, too many Christians walk in morbid fear of the power of Satan, and too many other Christians act (just as dangerously) as though he did not exist. Both are extreme errors to avoid, especially regarding the Worship of God.

It is obvious that Satan exists and retains at least a degree of power. Not only is this specifically taught in the New Testament, but it is seen throughout the ills of society. Indeed, most of the barriers to Worship we have already considered—from the increasingly fast pace of our culture to our lack of concentration and focus—have all been encouraged by the enemy. John Wesley went so far as to say that "all the works of our evil nature are the works of the devil."

Furthermore, it is to be assumed that Satan is utterly opposed to Christians Worshiping his enemy, our blessed Lord. Since Satan's job is to try to tempt us into forgetting God and His Law, he is doubtless frustrated when we do the opposite.

Nevertheless, we must not look at praise and worship (especially singing) as a kind of magic talisman that frightens the devil away. This is a very popular belief today, but it is never found in the Bible. There are many verses that command us to resist the devil, but none tells us to do so by singing. Consider a few:

> "Watch and pray so that you will not fall into temptation."
>
> Matthew 26:41

> Be on your guard; stand firm in the faith; be men of courage; be strong.
>
> 1 Corinthians 16:13

> Put on the full armor of God so that you can take your stand against the devil's schemes.
>
> Ephesians 6:11

> Resist the devil and he will flee from you.
>
> James 4:7

> Be self-controlled and alert. Your enemy the devil prowls around like a roaring lion looking for someone to devour. Resist him, standing firm in the faith.
>
> 1 Peter 5:8–9

If you believe that the devil is tempting you to sin, singing a song of praise may help if indeed it focuses your mind on Christ. But as we have seen from the very first, it is all too possible to be singing a Christian song while our minds are a thousand miles away.

It is not *music* that the devil hates (in fact, there is a lot of music in the world today that I am sure he enjoys and inspires!). The music of a praise song, that is, the technical sounds being made (the harmonic vocabulary, the physical vibrations, etc.) are not very different from the technical sounds of, shall we say, a secular love song. I do not think singing a secular love song like "Yesterday" by the Beatles will make the devil flee. (The way I might sing it would probably make people flee.) It is in the Christian words being sung or spoken with Christ's authority and their ability to focus us on the Lord that is repellent to our enemy. It is a *spiritual* battle we are waging, not a musical one. (More on this in the next chapter.)

The devil wants to keep us from Worshiping God, his arch-enemy. But Jesus' work has (fortunately for us) limited the devil's power so that his main weapons are trickery, fear and deception. Worship is not so much a weapon against Satan, per se—that is not the true function of Worshiping the Lord. One may duck into a church in order to avoid a sudden rainstorm, but that was not the reason the church was built. We Worship because of God and who He is, not because of Satan and who he is.

As well as repelling our enemy, true Worship is the perfect *preventative* against Satan's temptations. For if our eyes are focused on the face of the Lord, and "we take captive every thought to make it obedient to Christ" (2 Corinthians 10:5), a thousand devils could be at our backs and we would never even notice them, nor would they have the slightest power to harm us.

Other Barriers to Worship

There are other obstacles people face when trying to Worship God, but these listed affect the majority of us. We should never approach Worship as though we take it for granted that some obstacles will be along to hinder us. That is like waking up in the morning and assuming that we will get sick that day.

Our charge is to Worship the Lord. Since we know that God is even more desirous of this than we could ever be, let us, as the writer of Hebrews tells us, "then approach the throne of grace with confidence, so that we may receive mercy and find grace to help us in our time of need" (Hebrews 4:16).

In other words, let us begin by Worshiping God, not by looking out for obstacles. If indeed a barrier is discovered to hinder us, then let us deal with it as discussed and then get back to Worshiping. As stated so aptly by Brother Lawrence, "The world appears very little to a soul that contemplates the greatness of God. My business is to remain in the presence of God."

chapter seven

Music (and Other Arts) and Worship

Speak to one another with psalms, hymns and spiritual songs. Sing and make music in your heart to the Lord.

Ephesians 5:19

Whence hath the Church so many organs and musical instruments? To what purpose, I pray you, is that terrible blowing of bellows, expressing rather the cracks of thunder, than the sweetness of a voice?

Aelred, Abbot of Rievaultx

Music has been associated with worshiping God since the fourth chapter of the Bible, which mentions the first musician: "Jubal; he was the father of all who play the harp and the flute" (Genesis 4:21). Other arts have also been incorporated into worship from ancient times: dance, poetry, drama, painting, weaving, sculpting, architecture and many lesser art forms. Some of these, of course, have provoked controversy, but there are few believers who would not admit to some role of music and the arts in the practice of worship.

Although I personally believe that *all* arts should be used for God's glory, it must be admitted that music has the preeminent place in the history of Christian worship. Even today thousands of churches employ ministers of music for every one enlightened congregation that employs a "minister of arts." Rather than debate the justice or injustice of this preferential treatment, I will simply deal with music first—with my apologies to all the faithful Christian dancers, sculptors, and so on, throughout the world.

Since Christian music, in all its multitudinous forms, is so vastly popular in the Church today, we will spend some time examining its very essence. Later, we will examine its critical (and wonderful) use as a vehicle in worshiping God, and its specific use in private Worship, the central theme of this book.

What Is Christian Music?

Suppose we were to ask a number of different believers the question "What is Christian music?" The variety of responses might surprise you. For example, let us ask an orchestra conductor, a lay member of a small church, a professional violinist who is also a believer and the drummer in a Christian rock band.

The conductor: "Christian music is a popular misnomer for the term *sacred* music. It describes the vast amount of music in the classical repertoire, which uses voices (usually a chorus) singing a biblical or religious text. It includes such masterpieces as the

Bach *St. Matthew Passion,* Beethoven's *Missa Solemnis,* and the Brahms *Requiem."*

The parishioner: "Why, Christian music is what we sing every Sunday in church. The great hymns and anthems, the beautiful songs. Christian music is the music we use to worship God."

The Christian violinist: "As a Christian performer, I want every note I play to be for the glory of God. Whether I'm playing a string quartet or an arrangement of a hymn, I endeavor to infuse the music with the Spirit of God. Therefore, *everything* I play truly becomes a piece of Christian music, from a performing point of view."

The drummer: "Christian music is the music written since about 1960 by great songwriters and bands who want to take music back from the devil. We're tired of letting Satan have all the hit tunes. Finally, since the emergence of CCM [Contemporary Christian Music], artists are taking over the industry for Jesus."

Depending on your personal perspective, you probably smiled at some of these answers to the same question. (As one who has spent his life studying the history of music, I am particularly amused by the final one. It represents a huge body of fellow believers who seem to think that there was no Christian music between the times of the apostle Paul and Bill Gaither.)

Yet, which answer is correct? All of them? None of them?

Believers and Unbelievers—Sacred Versus Secular

Let's examine further. Whatever our musical tastes, I suppose that most of us could consider the following three examples as belonging somewhere within the realm of Christian music: the beautiful hymn *O Sacred Head Now Wounded,* a classical work for chorus and orchestra entitled *The Prodigal Son,* and a popular song by Christian singer Debbie Boone, *You Light Up My Life.*

Now look at these works in a different light. The old tune to *O Sacred Head* was originally a romantic love song sung by minstrels: "My Peace of Mind Is Shattered by a Tender Maiden's

Charms." (Try singing that some Sunday morning.) The Christian text was added years later. The fascinating work *The Prodigal Son* was written by composer Claude Debussy, an avowed atheist. And whatever the devout motives of Debbie Boone, a song like *You Light Up My Life* can easily be (and often is) sung as a love song to one's boy or girlfriend. The text never actually mentions the person who is lighting up your life!

The most bizarre of the three to modern Christians is probably the composition of a vocal work based on biblical text, as with the Debussy piece listed here. Actually, this was not an uncommon practice in some periods of music history—especially at times when the Church was interested in commissioning celebrated composers. Their personal beliefs were of no import; it was their musical talent that secured the jobs.

Composers in the Middle Ages and the Renaissance often copied earlier melodies—both sacred and secular—and put them together in their compositions. Sometimes they had different singers singing the vastly different melodies at the same time! For instance, in his mass *Faysans Regres,* the important composer Josquin de Pres (c. 1440–1521) mixed together a popular English tune with portions of Gregorian Chant written centuries earlier.

Many of the great masters were devout Christians but, of course, exceptions existed, and these musicians often composed sacred music along with their believing colleagues. The notorious atheist Hector Berlioz composed an exquisite work called *The Infancy of Christ*. His setting of these sacred scenes has stirred religious devotion in thousands of listeners. I defy anyone to hear it and "detect" a lack of faith—without previously being told!

Vocal Versus Instrumental

Let's go a step further. What about instrumental music? So far, though you may not have noticed it yet, we have implied that Christian music might be identified by its text. But is all Christian music necessarily *vocal?*

Consider a well-known and outspoken Christian composer such as Johann Sebastian Bach. One of his many masterpieces is a composition for chorus, soloists and orchestra; his text is based on the biblical account of Jesus' Passion. He entitled the work *Passion According to St. Matthew*. Doubtless we can all agree that this is an example of Christian music.

But what if Bach composed an instrumental piece for harpsichord, chamber ensemble or baroque orchestra. Should these works also be considered in the realm of Christian music? Before you answer negatively, it should be noted that Bach himself would have answered in the affirmative. He insisted that all of his music was written to glorify God. Many other composers throughout the centuries have made similar claims.

Whether vocal or purely instrumental, Bach made no distinction between "sacred" and "secular." For instance, at the beginning of such a "secular" work as his "Little Organ Book," he wrote this dedication: "To God alone the praise be given for what's herein to man's use written." His "Little Clavier Book," like so many of his compositions, was inscribed *In Nomine Jesu* ("In the Name of Jesus"). For many other such examples in classical music, see my book *Spiritual Lives of Great Composers* (Zondervan, 1996).

Or suppose someone takes a well-known Christian song— perhaps a hymn with text clearly identifying it as Christian— and then plays it instrumentally. Is it still Christian music if no words are sung? Could someone who had never heard of this song have any inkling of its spirituality? I rather doubt it.

Yet dozens of Christian music companies produce instrumental CDs of the great hymns and other works. Would any of us listen to "Praise Strings" recordings and not consider it Christian music?

And what about titles? Does a Christian title on a work make it Christian music? Suppose I wrote a piano piece and called it "Sunrise." Then I later decided to change the title to "Easter Morning." Has my piano piece now been born again?

Many composers, such as the French master Olivier Messiaen, place programmatic titles of a Christian nature on their instrumental works. This composer considered such pieces unquestionably "Christian music." Suppose you heard his beautiful organ solo *The Nativity of the Lord* without knowing the title. Would you discern its spiritual intent? Suppose he had written the exact same notes and given it a secular title—or a Hindu or New Age title?

What Is *Music*?

Before you read this chapter, you probably thought you knew exactly what Christian music was. Now you may be wondering *what* to believe! In order to clarify an issue, it is helpful to look at it from a number of new and different angles.

I have deliberately muddied the waters so that we might be forced to examine terminology, which is used rather loosely today within so-called Christian music. Now we can begin to sort out the matter.

Rather than ask the question "What is Christian music?" I want to ask a more basic one: "What is *music?*" I do not mean this in the technical, acoustical or theoretical sense. Nor am I referring to such elements as rhythm, melody, harmony, form. I mean simply, "What are the most basic components of the music most people listen to?"

Music and Words: Separate Elements

The key was hinted at earlier. Every piece of music written since the dawn of time can be categorized into one of two primary divisions: vocal music and instrumental music. The former incorporates music and words; the latter only music. Music and words then, as separate items, are the two basic components of a given composition.

This rather obvious fact is often obscured today, probably because popular songwriters compose both the music and the

142

lyrics for their songs. The words and the music seem intricately intertwined, as, of course, they should be in well-written vocal music. But it is almost as if the Christian message of the text somehow sanctifies the music itself, so that we seem to have Christian melodies, Christian harmonic progressions, maybe even Christian rhythms!

This confusion between music and words has not always existed. Martin Luther, who wrote both music and prose, believed fervently that "next to the Word of God, music deserves the highest praise." But he made clear distinction between words and music, as he taught that God had given us language in order that we could "praise God with both word and music, namely, by proclaiming the Word of God through music and by providing sweet melodies with words."

Throughout the centuries of classical music, this "music versus words" concept was clear. Most of the vocal music composed by the great masters used words written by other people, often great poets. Even when Wagner innovatively wrote both the music and the texts to his *Ring of the Nibelung* cycle of four operas, the two were studied separately. Musicologists still refer to Wagner the composer as well as Wagner the poet.

Two Very Different Examples

To illustrate in a humorous light the detachment of words and music, I will take you back a few decades to my boyhood. Many other children of the 1950s and '60s will remember—with some embarrassment—a popular television show called *Gilligan's Island*. They may recall its catchy theme song, with its sublime text ("Now this is a tale of our castaways, they're here for a long, long time . . .").

Imagine my incredulity when I arrived to pick up my teenage son from his church youth group and heard them singing—with great gusto and sincerity—this very theme song to the words of "Amazing Grace"! Try it sometime, preferably when no one is around.

143

I really have no idea of the faith (or lack thereof) of the composer of the *Gilligan's Island* theme song. But I rather doubt that his motive was to create a worship song to be sung at church. It was certainly not "Christian music" in its creation, though my son triumphantly claims that it has "now been redeemed."

Let us try another example and travel in the other direction. Take the best-written and most beloved Christian song you can think of, one in which words and music are skillfully united. Let us remove the Christian lyrics and give this instrumental work to an equally skilled lyricist from a country such as Egypt. He can carefully superimpose an effective lyric to this music that invokes its listeners to worship Allah.

Again I ask: "Is this *still* a Christian song?" For anyone who might be tempted to answer in the affirmative, I would then ask, "If this song, with its new Moslem lyrics, remains a Christian song, would you want to sing it this Sunday at church?" I don't recommend it.

No. It is certainly no longer a Christian song, even though the music itself was untouched. Only the words have changed, and that is all that is necessary for its character to be changed.

The only thing that makes a Christian song *Christian* is its Christian words.

Not the music. The music has nothing to do with it. It may be excellently or terribly written music; that is not the issue. As Augustine stated about sacred music, "It is *the setting for the words* which give it life."

This in no way belittles the wonderful music that has been written by Christian composers throughout the ages. Thousands of composers (including myself) have written millions of compositions for the purpose of glorifying God and edifying fellow believers. I am not trying to detract from or to applaud the worth of Christian music but simply to clarify what it is.

A song may be an excellent Christian song or a terrible Christian song; it may be an excellent Muslim song or a terrible Muslim song. Whether it is excellent or terrible depends on the talent of the composer. Whether it is Christian or not depends only on its lyrics.

If you ponder this long enough, I think you will come to the same conclusion.

Ramifications

This being the case, what do we draw from this understanding?

To begin with, it means that only vocal music can ever be considered as Christian music. The greatest instrumental masterpieces—whether written by devout masters like Bach or contemporary Christian artists—are masterpieces of *music*. Without texts there is nothing Christian about them that could be detected by anyone unfamiliar with the composers' beliefs or intentions.

Even biblical titles do not help. If someone listened to an instrumental work without first being told the Christian title, nothing in the music itself would necessarily suggest any particular spirituality.

Therefore, the *melody* to such a famous hymn as "Amazing Grace" is not a Christian melody. If you perform it instrumentally—even an instrumental verse between sung verses—it only seems like Christian music to us because the melody *reminds* us of the Christian text we have heard many times before. We can worship effectively with it because of its longstanding connection with John Newton's powerful story of God's amazing grace.

I suspect that this is the answer to the interesting passage of 2 Kings 3:15, where Elisha summons a harpist and then receives the word of the Lord. This is often cited as an example of instrumental music that seemed to be "heavenly" or "sacred" in itself. It is equally possible, however, that the instrumental music reminded him of the great songs of Zion and put him in a frame of mind to hear clearly from the Lord.

Music can indeed be a tremendous aid to worship, but it is still the words themselves that give clarity to our Christian beliefs. This was cleverly pointed out in the fourth century by Basil,

145

Bishop of Caesarea. He explained that the Holy Spirit "blends the delight of music with the truth of doctrine, in order that through the pleasantness and beauty of the sounds we might unawares receive what is useful in the words, according to the practice of wise physicians, who, when they give the more bitter draughts to the sick, often smear the rim of the cup with honey."

Ultimately, then, there is no such thing as Christian music any more than there are Christian chords or Christian rhythms or Christian melodic intervals. There are only Christian words, combined with music, pure and simple.

(Conversely, there are no "demonic chords" or "demonic rhythms" either, despite the fashionable claims of those who have not carefully studied the point. The reason that some types of instrumental music may sound "demonic" to many is because these sounds remind us of music with lyrics that are indeed worldly or worse.)

What is generally called Christian music today is a combination of two art forms: music and Christian poetry. It is not unusual to combine art forms; both opera and theater, for example, combine several different arts. The reason we must separate words and music in Christian music is to show exactly what makes it "Christian." And it is never the music itself.

But Doesn't Music Communicate?

Musical laymen have always loved to wax eloquent on the supposed communicative value of music, but no one who spends hours composing instrumental music is very impressed. The great composers, who spend their lives working with notes as a carpenter works with wood, have few romantic notions of the "meaning of music." If they want to communicate with someone they use words, not ambiguous musical notes.

Igor Stravinsky, perhaps the greatest classical composer of the twentieth century, explained that "all music is nothing more than a succession of impulses that converge toward a definite point of repose." Charles Ives, considered by many musicologists to be America's first master composer, gave us a typically confused answer on the subject: "Music—that no one knows what it is—and the less he knows what it is the nearer it is to music—probably." Incidentally, both of these brilliant composers were strong, outspoken Christians.

Conductors, who must interpret instrumental music, have no illusions about exact communications through music without words. Renowned British conductor Sir Thomas Beecham stated flatly: "The plain fact is that music *per se* means nothing; it is sheer sound." This does not mean that music cannot communicate at all. It communicates pathos, passions and a huge array of feelings—from desolation to exhilaration. But these are oblique and subjective, far more vague even than the medium of words.

Therefore, the study of Christian music is the study of any vocal music *using Christian texts* that has been composed in the last two thousand years. It may be superb music; it may be mediocre or even horrible music. It may be composed by believers or unbelievers. It may bring us into a state of ecstatic worship of God; it may make us wonder why we ever bought that CD player for our son in the first place. But it is Christian music if and only if it uses Christian words.

Paul's Musical Directive

What about Paul's admonition to "sing psalms, hymns and spiritual songs"? What do these terms mean? They appear twice in the New Testament, in Ephesians 5:19 and Colossians 3:16. It is most likely that Paul was simply describing the music possibilities for any given worship service.

The first two terms are not so difficult to understand. *Psalms* obviously refers to various psalms from the Hebrew Scriptures. And the Greek word *Hymnis* means "a song written in praise or honor of God." That is, a piece of vocal music *in which the text* praises or honors God. It could have been composed by King

David or by the local songwriter. Most of the millions of Christian songs we know today could fit into this very broad category.

Paul's *spiritual songs* has provoked much speculation, however, often bordering on musical and theological lunacy. This term, which is sometimes translated "spiritual odes" or "spiritual canticles," is neither mystical nor magical. Perhaps in mentioning both "hymns" and "odes" in his listing, Paul used the latter term to cover the improvised songs (possibly combined with ecstatic tongues) that were an integral part of the worship service. This may also include "singing with the spirit," which he mentions in his first letter to the Corinthians (see 1 Corinthians 14:15).

Whatever their precise meanings, there is nothing either in the Scriptures or in music history to indicate some special "Christian music" by the words *psalms, hymns and spiritual songs*. The emphasis is clearly on the text itself, not the actual music: A "psalm" means that the text is from the Psalms; a "hymn" means that the text praises or honors God; a "spiritual song" means a song in which the text is of a spiritual nature. Whether or not you believe that the music itself is "spiritual" is purely subjective.

Christian Symbols: Non-Musical Art Forms and Worship

Since we understand that words can be specifically Christian, let us consider those art forms that utilize words for their basic materials, such as literature and poetry. Some things are obvious: When one writes a story about a Christian topic, such as "Christ's Victory Over Satan," it can be called a "Christian story." Likewise, if one writes a story about something rather non-Christian (not necessarily anti-Christian), such as "How to Raise a Ferret," it can be called a "secular story."

Of course, there may be those who insist that the ferret story is really Christian, too, since it involves one of God's little creatures (maybe the ferret was even baptized!) or some similarly obscure argument. But for our purposes we will keep it simple.

148

Either the art form specifically uses Christian words or we will consider it to be secular.

What about the many other art forms that, like music, also do not use words? If there is no such thing as Christian music, then is there no such thing as Christian painting? Or architecture? Or sculpture? Do we discount Rembrandt's *Christ Descending from the Cross* or Michelangelo's *Pieta* as secular because they do not use Christian words?

No. They use Christian *symbols* and *images,* which are equally as valid as Christian words. For example, if an architect designs a building in the shape of a cross, this is an obvious example of Christian architecture even though no Christian words are involved.

So let us clarify one final time. Music—pure music, instrumental music—uses neither words nor images nor any true Christian symbols. Only sounds. Only pitches placed in certain relationships to each other in time, that is, in rhythmic patterns. This is why composer Igor Stravinsky insisted that "music is far closer to mathematics than to literature."

Therefore, we have no more reason to talk of Christian music than Christian cardboard. Like cardboard—which could be made into a cross or into a satanic symbol—the sounds of music can be constructed into many different guises. It is the Christian *words* or *symbols* employed by the different arts that make them distinctively Christian arts.

The Place of Beauty in Worship

How does all of this categorizing affect our topic of Worship? A great deal.

Let us take an example that occurs at hundreds of churches every Sunday morning. You walk in from the vestibule and a musician is playing an instrumental version of a great Christian song. The sounds inspire you and prod you to worship the Lord. Why?

As we have seen, it may be because you know this song and hearing it instrumentally reminds you of its great Christian words. But suppose you have never heard this song. Well, perhaps the style of the music reminds you of other Christian songs, and this reminds you of the great Christian words within these songs.

Maybe. But there is another explanation. When you are inspired to worship God after hearing an instrumental prelude it is not because of either Christian words or Christian symbols. It is because of its *beauty*.

In the second chapter, we saw how God uses our natural love of beauty and order to draw us to Himself. This is because beauty is an intrinsic aspect of our Lord, of His own nature. When the Scriptures invite us to "gaze upon the beauty of the LORD" (Psalm 27:4), the word *beauty* describes—*literally* describes—God Himself.

Now we can go further than before. The second chapter taught us that: "When we sing God's praises in a fine song with skillful accompaniment, when we marvel at the beauty of our churches (architecture, banners, vestments), when we are moved by beautiful and meaningful prayers—God uses these external motivators in order to open the way for something internal to happen."

This is the truest purpose for music (and other arts) in worship: to display and signify the beauty of God. This is not a new concept in history. Music and beauty were associated by the great thinkers of old. Plato claimed that "the business of music should in some manner lead us to the love of the beautiful." This concept would be taken up by many of the early Church Fathers, and contemplated extensively by Augustine and later by Thomas Aquinas.

Yet surely we now see that beauty is found in many avenues other than "Christian Arts." We can now add to the previous paragraph: When you see a breathtaking sunset, when you marvel at the beauty of a mountain range, when you thrill at walking through a picturesque forest—God is using these externals in order to have something internal happen between you and your Creator.

"All right," you concede. "Perhaps you could use these beautiful scenes from nature to inspire your worship of God. But of course, He created all these scenes. They are almost like the great Christian music of our church, as far as their ability to encourage worship."

Yes, they are, because of their beauty and the way that their beauty reminds us of the beauty of God. But if it is their beauty—and not some Christian words or symbols—that makes them so efficacious in awakening worship within us, what about other things (even man-made things) that contain beauty?

Using Non-Christian Arts to Worship the Lord?!

This may astound some Christians, but one can worship God just as easily and effectually with a beautiful symphony as with a beautiful hymn. In fact, for many of us who were not raised with hymns but with symphonies, they may be more effective and appropriate for use in arousing worship. This is true even though the symphony contains neither Christian words nor symbols, and may not even have been written by a Christian composer.

The reason is beauty. Surely we would rather listen to an instrumental piece composed by a skilled non-Christian than one composed by an unskilled Christian. Why? Because the skilled composer will give us a piece of music containing greater beauty and, therefore, one that more closely resembles "the beauty of the Lord."

We can state this more easily. Would you rather take your malfunctioning car to a skilled non-Christian mechanic or to a Christian who, unfortunately, knows little about fixing cars? The choice is obvious. You may have better fellowship with the latter. He may even pray for God's help in the repair work. But what you want from a mechanic is the orderliness (or the beauty) of an accurate repair job. The same is true of doctors, artists or those in any other occupation that requires skill. (Actually, all occupations do.)

Consider the ultimate symbol for worship in the Old Testament: the Temple. Did not God use unbelievers for its construction? Perhaps there were some legalists who objected when David brought cedar logs from the Sidonians and Tyrians (see 1 Chronicles 22:4) and when Solomon sent to the Gentile King of Tyre for skilled workers (see 2 Chronicles 2:7). But the Bible records no such scruples, and there is no indication whatsoever that God disapproved.

So if a beautiful string quartet fills you with feelings of rapture, praise God for it! If a magnificent painting inspires you to worship the Lord, do it with all your might! Do not feel guilty because it is not a Christian hymn. It is the Lord Himself who ultimately placed beauty within it, and His reason was to draw you closer to Him.

A Word of Caution

Consider again why God created beauty: to draw us closer to Him, the Creator. Unfortunately, this is not how the world generally reacts to beauty. Instead of seeing beauty as a means toward worshiping God, too many begin to worship the object of beauty itself.

Paul describes such practice in Romans 1:25: "They exchanged the truth of God for a lie, and worshiped and served created things rather than the Creator—who is forever praised. Amen."

In Augustine's *Confessions*, we find this dilemma was painfully acute. He loved sacred music but wrote: "So I waver between the danger that gratifying the senses and the benefits which, as I know from experience, can accrue from singing." These scruples did not keep him from songs of praise, but he admitted: "Yet when I find the singing itself more moving than the truth it conveys, I confess that this is a grievous sin, and at those times I prefer not to hear the singer."

Do you remember the analogy of the "introducer" from the second chapter? The idea was that beauty was created in order to introduce us to God, almost like a good hostess who brings you to meet someone, then exits to leave the two of you alone.

But suppose that instead of staying to get to know your new acquaintance, all your attention remains on the lovely hostess. You follow her everywhere, much to her annoyance, and ignore the guest you were to meet and get to know.

This is exactly what the world has done all too often with the beauty God has given us, whether natural or man-made beauty. Instead of praising the Lord for it (and through it), people have focused on the beauty itself. They study it, analyze it, go to lectures about it, indeed, worship it—and God is left on the outside, unrecognized, unappreciated and unworshiped. This is a modern descendant of the idolatry of old.

Christians and the Beauty of the Arts

Unfortunately, this idolatrous practice by the world has led many sincere Christians to abandon the arts as "worldly." Perhaps they fear that they, too, will succumb to worshiping the beauty itself and forget about God, but this is a gross overreaction. One might as well be afraid to put a foot in the ocean because "others have drowned in it"!

Why not simply learn to swim? Why not learn to worship God for (and through) the beauty He has given us for this actual purpose? Instead of avoiding art in fear and ignorance, why not revel in the beauty of God's creative nature—regardless of the folly of the world?

When my wife and I walk through an outstanding art gallery, we are inwardly (and often outwardly!) praising the Lord for the beauty we are being allowed to see. When we hear or perform in a great symphony, we are deeply inspired to worship God for the joy and passion of the music we are experiencing.

It comes from the Lord—not from Beethoven, not from Monet, not from Michelangelo. They were the vessels God used to create through, and perhaps they are imperfect ones

153

like ourselves. But any beauty that enters our senses and pierces our hearts comes from the ultimate Creator. Indeed, Michelangelo himself maintained, "I live and love in God's peculiar light."

James sums this up for us: "Every good and perfect gift *is from above,* coming down from the Father of the heavenly lights, who does not change like shifting shadows" (James 1:17, emphasis added). God has given us magnificent beauty in music and the arts, and He expects us to use it (not ignore it) to His glory. For Jesus admonishes us: "From everyone who has been given much, much will be demanded; and from the one who has been entrusted with much, much more will be asked" (Luke 12:48).

Practical Applications for Private Worship

How can we use the beauty of music and the other arts and the beauty found in nature to help us Worship the Lord? Let us start with a bit of sorting. To begin with, we all have unique tastes, likes and dislikes. We should first identify those sources of beauty that we already appreciate; perhaps others can be added later with a little effort.

Rather than divide up the arts into categories and further categorize various beauties found in nature, let us simply ask ourselves a few key questions. Do you like to

- watch a sunset?
- listen to a great CCM singer?
- thumb through an art book of the great masters?
- hear a sublime symphony?
- walk through a forest?
- sing a hymn?
- read a book of poetry?
- listen to Gregorian Chant?
- see one of Shakespeare's plays?

This list could go on and on, and if your favorite pursuit of beauty is not yet listed, please go ahead and identify it in your mind.

Some of you may be thinking, "These are wonderful things to do, but how do they help me to worship God? Especially, how do such ideas help me to privately Worship God? How could I privately Worship God while watching a Shakespeare play?"

Answer: You don't have to bring your Worship time into the theater while the play is being acted before you. But you might want to *bring the inspiration* of the play (or sunset, or song, or painting, or symphony, or hymn, or poem) back into your quiet time.

Some Examples

In my quiet times of Worshiping the Lord, when my natural attention begins to wane, I might bring to mind the memory of

- a beautiful sunset
- a passage from Shakespeare's *Henry V* (when the king prays for courage the night before the battle of Agincourt)
- a hymn I learned in childhood
- a Rembrandt painting
- a Bach cantata
- a poem by George Herbert

As these memories come to the surface, I begin anew to Worship God and praise Him for the beauty He has given us. Notice that I have not brought any externals into the time of my Worship. These are simply memories stored away to inspire me in my Worship of the Lord. The more I have, the more I can utilize for this wonderful purpose.

Furthermore, we should try to surround our daily quiet times with elements of beauty. When possible, I like to have mine outside, preferably away from man-made buildings. A park, a forest, a garden—anything that might remind us of the beauty of the Lord. Then we carry God's beauty back within us when we leave. It reminds me of the words of Ralph Waldo Emerson: "Fear God, and where you go men will think they walk in hallowed cathedrals."

Obviously, there are times when no outward beauty is available. Then we must draw on what is internal to help us. When Corrie ten Boom was locked in solitary confinement during World War II, she rose every morning and sang a hymn to her Lord. She used the music and the Christian poetry that was within her to Worship God, even in the most unbeautiful of situations.

God gave us natural beauty—the beauty of music and the arts—and our own talents and abilities to remember the beauty we experience. These were given to us, as Bach would remind his students, for two basic reasons: to glorify God and to edify us. Both of these purposes are realized simultaneously when we use these gifts to Worship the Lord.

chapter eight

Charismatic and Non-Charismatic Worship

What then shall we say, brothers? When you come together, everyone has a hymn, or a word of instruction, a revelation, a tongue or an interpretation. All of these must be done for the strengthening of the church.

1 Corinthians 14:26

Divine inspirations are not, like the diabolical possessions of heathen priests, violent and ungovernable, and prompting them to act as if they were beside themselves; but are sober and calm, capable of regular conduct. The man inspired by the Spirit of God may still act the man, and observe the rules of natural order and decency in delivering his revelations. His spiritual life is thus far subject to his pleasure, and to be managed by his discretion.

Matthew Henry

This is perhaps the most contentious issue today among the worshiping Christian Church. Thousands of sincere, Bible-believing Christians are in total disagreement on this subject, and there seems no end in sight to the unremitting quarrel. If Martians had landed on earth in the first century, read 1 Corinthians 14, left and returned today, they might ask us in wonder: "You haven't figured this out yet?"

In the big picture of one's Christian walk, it should not be a major issue. For that matter, taking the entire Bible with its 1,189 chapters, the few chapters from the book of Acts and 1 Corinthians that deal with the charismatic gifts are a rather small portion. Hundreds of books about Christianity and the Christian life are written each year that do not even mention the subject.

But to write a book about worship, whether corporate or private worship, means to run head-on into this controversy. An author usually accepts one of two options: (1) You write about worship within the "side you are on" and ignore the other side as though it did not exist, or (2) You write about your side and openly condemn the worship practices of the other side.

I am taking neither of these well-trodden paths. I will instead take the dangerous and perhaps unpopular path of blessing both camps, condemning neither, and even trying to discover how Christians on both sides of this issue can learn from one another. If you are willing to take such a path, it may mean questioning some of the things you have heard for most of your Christian life, including many sermons in your own church. You may or may not change your views on charismatic doctrines—and I am not suggesting that you should—but at least you will learn about life on the other side and, we can all hope, abandon any condemnation of fellow believers.

Whose *Side* Are You On?

Every time I have mentioned to various Christian leaders that I am writing a book about worship, I am immediately asked the question "Which type, charismatic or not?" I have lost count of how many times I have been asked this question. My answer, "Neither," invites puzzled looks so I add, "Just read the book." This chapter is the real answer to the question.

First of all, it should be noted that there are many more than two "worship styles" in the Church today. Do you remember all the variations encountered by the fanciful angel in the beginning of the first chapter? Perhaps you feel that your church cannot correctly be put into one of two molds.

You are right, of course. I am not trying to place every church in the world today into one of only two categories. But it is surely obvious that on the topic of worship, the charismatic versus non-charismatic issues are very much on the forefront of debate. It is time to see if the two sides can come together in peace instead of argument. Paul thus exhorts us: "Let us therefore make every effort to do what leads to peace and to mutual edification" (Romans 14:19).

Many outstanding preachers and Christian leaders are on each side on the charismatic battle. Many denominations are clearly on one side or the other, while a few brave ones are split—with both charismatic and non-charismatic services. The largest para-church ministries as well are informally known to be "rather charismatic" or "rather non-charismatic."

The Church has become amazingly polarized on this issue, and we are each expected to cast our votes squarely for one side or the other. It is almost like the Republicans and the Democrats, both of whom look down with disdain on the Independents; it is safer to be a loyal member of either side. Likewise, for many years in Northern Ireland it was a fairly safe and protected position to be clearly in one camp or the other; the innocents who were not against either faction were often attacked by both sides for their neutrality.

Why Did You Choose Your Church?

Have you ever thought about the question "Why does one *become* a charismatic?" For that matter, we could ask, "Why does one *become* a Baptist or a Presbyterian or whatever?" Perhaps an easier way to deal with such questions is to ask yourself: "Why do I go to my church or denomination?"

It may surprise you to find that the reason most Christians today are in a certain church or denomination is either:

1. They were raised in that church (or denomination) from childhood.
2. They came to Christ later in life and were encouraged to go to that church (or denomination) by those who brought them to Christ.

Most of us fit into one of these two categories and there is nothing whatsoever wrong with this. But this means that very few of us ever really sat down and said to ourselves something like: "Now, I'm a Christian, and I believe a Christian should go to church. So I'm going to forget about my background and upbringing and look at the Bible and find a church that seems best to fit the biblical pattern."

A few free thinkers among us have made such deliberate decisions, but for most of us this was not the case. If we were in the first category listed above, the decision was really made by our parents and we simply continued with it. If we were in the second category, the decision was basically made by those who brought us to Christ.

By this, I do not mean looking for a new church when you move to a new town. I mean that, if you are a Lutheran, would you consider becoming a member of a Methodist church? If you are in the Church of Christ, would you consider becoming a member of an Assemblies of God church? If not, why not?

The two answers that are usually given to that question are:

1. Loyalty—that is, why should you suddenly leave the church you have been attending for some time? Obviously, this is a good and admirable answer.

2. Style—that is, you would not feel comfortable at that other church; their worship style doesn't fit your personality. Considering all that we have already seen about our unique personalities, this answer is also understandable.

Why We Feel the Way We Do

Nothing is intrinsically wrong with either answer, but this does point out a problem. Neither answer is quite as satisfactory as something like: "I have personally examined the Scriptures and prayed fervently to find the church that I believe best conforms to the biblical pattern. The reason I go to this church (or denomination) is because *I truly believe* in the doctrine taught here."

And, of course, we all hasten to agree with such words. We really *do* believe in the doctrines of our church. (At least, I hope so!) But how did we come to believe in them? For many of us, sitting Sunday after Sunday for many years in the same church became rather comfortable. Long ago we began to take on this church's doctrine as our own. Again, please understand that there is nothing wrong with this.

But now, consider the charismatic issue. Let us ask a question of two different groups of readers.

For those readers who are charismatics, consider: If you had been raised in a non-charismatic church (or were brought as a new Christian to a non-charismatic church) and fed years of non-charismatic teaching, would you perhaps still be there today?

For those readers who are not charismatics, consider: If you had been raised in a charismatic church (or were brought as a new Christian to a charismatic church) and fed years of charismatic teaching, would you perhaps still be there today?

We need to be completely honest with ourselves. As Thomas á Kempis reminds us, "A humble knowledge of oneself is a surer way to God than a deep search after knowledge." For most of us, if past circumstances had been different, we might be in a completely different situation today.

And do you know what? It would not be such a terrible thing after all. Believe it or not, there are many wonderful people in *all* the different denominations, charismatic and non-charismatic alike. This fact alone should help us to resist condemning those outside our churches or denominations.

For those who might demur with the objection "I could never be comfortable with the way they worship in such and such denomination," let me answer, "Perhaps you could, in time." Literally every personality type is found in every Christian church. That's right, there are even some *quiet* charismatics. I have met many of them.

Doctrinal Issues Versus Worship Styles

Notice that so far we have emphasized the different worship styles rather than the doctrines found within different churches. That is, I submit that if you are, say, a Presbyterian, you could begin going to, say, a Baptist church service and *after a time* you could actually get used to it and finally be quite comfortable there. The same is true for all of the principal denominations of the Christian faith, or at least within Protestant denominations.

Nevertheless, it is one thing to "get used to" a different style of worship. It is quite another matter to change in the area of doctrine. Concerning these essential matters of our personal faith, Paul is very clear: "Each one should be fully convinced in his own mind" (Romans 14:5).

The reason I bring all this to the surface is to consider the charismatic question from two distinct viewpoints: (1) charismatic worship styles and (2) charismatic doctrine.

It is common to say, "You can't separate the two!" But as we shall see, not only can we, but *most churches do so every Sunday!* That is, there are hundreds of excellent churches that balk at charismatic doctrine yet embrace charismatic worship styles.

This really is true. My ministry takes me to many churches and denominations. It has been fascinating to see how many churches of every flavor have been influenced by the charismatic renewal.

I recently taught in a large church in our Washington, D.C., area that is known to be a bulwark of non-charismatic teaching. Yet their corporate worship was amazingly similar to that of the charismatic churches nearby. All the songs they sang came from charismatic circles, for instance, and the only difference from a charismatic worship service I could see was that there were no outbreaks of either prophecy or speaking in tongues.

This could never have happened in that church twenty years ago. (I even saw a man in the back raise his hands! Horrors!) The pastor, who still preaches strongly against the charismatic renewal, never used to allow "that charismatic music" in his church. And yet it is used there and in hundreds of non-charismatic churches today. Why?

Because of the difference between charismatic worship styles and charismatic doctrine. One can completely repudiate the essence of charismatic doctrine but still effectively employ many of its worship practices. Let us consider a few of these.

Charismatic Music?

This leads us to the ridiculous question "What is charismatic music?" Is it music in which the singer breaks out in tongues? Does he write down such speaking in tongues for copyright purposes?

Obviously, there is nothing particularly "charismatic"—employing the charismatic gifts, such as tongues or prophecy—about the genre of praise music, which is often categorized as charismatic music. Having analyzed dozens of these songs I can assure you that, *from a purely musical point of view*, there is nothing especially different that could separate them from any other type of worship song, including classic hymns.

For charismatic readers, I am afraid I must say that there is nothing "extra-spiritual" or "anointed" about the music of these songs.

For non-charismatic readers, I can assure you that there is nothing "harmful" or "demonic" about the music of these songs.

163

Please do not misunderstand me: This is not to belittle the wonderful quality of praise songs or their ability to be used for edifying God's people. They are, however, simply Christian songs that happen to be composed by Christians within the charismatic renewal. Can these songs be used effectively in non-charismatic churches? Certainly.

(Again, notice that we must separate the music from *the words*, as we learned in the previous chapter. A non-charismatic pastor may choose to reject a charismatic song because of its words, that is, its theology. But to do so because of the music itself? Well, as we saw a chapter ago, if there is no such thing as Christian music, there is no such thing as charismatic music!)

Charismatic Lingo?

Consider another issue. In most charismatic churches, it is quite common for individuals to repeat certain phrases and snatches of Scripture: "Praise God. Thank You, Jesus. Glory to Your name, O God. We love You, Lord. You're worthy of praise. Praise to You, Jesus."

This practice often drives non-charismatics crazy, especially if it takes place when someone else is praying. They consider it uncouth, inappropriate, disrespectful. Most of all, they consider that it sounds so *charismatic*.

But is there anything charismatic about this? Are any of the charismatic gifts involved? No. Are any of these phrases unscriptural or anti-scriptural? Of course not. Is there any scriptural reason that a non-charismatic could not say the same phrases? None whatsoever.

Then why don't they? Style, not doctrine. There is no real doctrinal issue here. It is simply a question of style, of what you are used to, and of what feels comfortable to you because of your background.

"Stylistic" questions have always risen in the Body of Christ, and fortunately they have not always been a cause for conflict. A classic example concerned fasting. Augustine wrote Ambrose to ask advice about fasting while he was traveling to different cities that had diverse customs on the subject. Ambrose's famous answer has been paraphrased throughout the ages: "When I am at Rome, I fast on a Saturday; when I am in Milan, I do not. Do the same. Follow the custom of the church where you are."

Such liberty could also be applied to the practice of raising one's hands in church. This is very common in charismatic churches but not in non-charismatic ones. Why? Again, style, not doctrine. Surely no pastor—even one strongly anti-charismatic—could find a doctrinal reason not to raise one's hands. It is clearly found in Scripture. Those who do not employ this "charismatic" practice do so because it does not fit in with *the style* of their non-charismatic churches.

The Real Problem Areas

Many practices, loosely identified with charismatic worship, really have nothing to do with charismatic doctrine. As we have seen from the above examples, practices such as singing a certain style of music, saying a certain type of lingo, lifting your hands or even dancing in the church are only "charismatic" by association—and even these are far from being universal within the charismatic renewal.

What worship practices, then, are truly charismatic? The word *charismatic* comes from the Greek word for *gift,* referring to the spiritual gifts listed in several places in the New Testament. The primary passage in which this concept is discussed at length is in 1 Corinthians 12–14.

For instance, in 1 Corinthians 12:28–30, Paul lists a number of these gifts or people who have received such gifts:

- apostles
- prophets
- teachers

165

- workers of miracles
- gifts of healing
- gifts of helping
- gifts of administration
- gifts of speaking in tongues

Of these eight gifts, three are in virtually every type of Christian church: teachers, those with gifts of helping and those with gifts of administration. The position of apostle is somewhat disputed in most churches today. At any rate, it has little to do with worship and does not enter into our discussion.

Another controversy I purposely choose to avoid concerns the workers of miracles and the gifts of healing. Some might consider these, like that of apostles, as having little to do with worship and, therefore, outside our discussion. But there are many charismatics who believe that healing miracles take place within (and because of) corporate worship services. Nevertheless, since this book is primarily concerned with private Worship—in which healing and miracles are not an essential factor—we will not let this controversy distract us.

What then is left in this list of gifts? Prophecy and speaking in tongues. These two functions mark the critical differences between the typical charismatic church and non-charismatic church. That is, these are two things that will never occur at a non-charismatic worship service.

Tongues: The "Die-on-Your-Sword" Difference

Perhaps the last sentence is a bit too strong. Regarding prophecy at least. It is true that in the many non-charismatic churches I have visited, I have never heard anyone begin a classic thunderous prophecy: "Thus saith the Lord. . . ."

But I have frequently heard an interesting "translation" of this concept. Even the most anti-charismatic preachers are often heard using phrases such as:

166

"I believe God is leading us to . . ."
"I felt that the Lord was saying to . . ."
"I believe that God directed me to . . ."

Do you see the point? Many non-charismatics who would never endorse "prophecy" do believe in some form of divine guidance. They would never say, "Thus saith the Lord," but they would pray for the Lord's direction in their lives and expect Him to answer somehow. Although their "prophecies" are not as demonstrative and explicit, the concept of "God speaking to His people" is not at all unknown to non-charismatics.

But tongues are another matter. On this one issue above all others, the charismatics and non-charismatics will always disagree. From the viewpoint of Christian worship practices, this is the very heart of the disagreement.

Why do tongues create such notorious antagonism? Theologians have given us many reasons, but it seems that two always rise to the surface:

1. Because speaking in tongues is an absolutely otherworldly, unnatural experience. That is, there is really nothing else in natural living that is similar to speaking in tongues. The concept of prophecy may be unusual, but at least it involves human words with which we are all familiar. But speaking in another language—perhaps a heavenly or angelic language—and not even understanding what you are saying? Even those who do this every day must admit that the idea sounds incomprehensible to the uninitiated.

2. Because, if speaking in tongues is *not* what the charismatics believe—that is, if it is not a heavenly language inspired by God—then the alternatives for what occurs are not very pleasant. Ask the non-charismatics, "If what happens isn't speaking in tongues, then what is it?" Even the kindest will often refer to motor automatism, states of hypnosis or

ecstasy, learned behavior or even demonic activity. One can easily imagine how the faithful charismatic reacts to such a diagnosis!

United in Worship or Declaring War?

My book is certainly not going to untie this Gordian knot that the greatest theologians of the centuries have disagreed about. Nor is it this book's purpose. I would never ask you to change your fundamental doctrines, but I would ask you to have understanding of those whom you disagree with. I have tried to demonstrate how the two camps are not quite as far apart—at least in terms of worship styles—as is commonly supposed. Nevertheless, the war continues.

I feel compelled to make a short digression from this book's topics and goals to make a plea for peace on this issue. Many pastors feel under some obligation to defend their theological positions by attacking the differing positions of others. In the meantime, God is not being worshiped and the Gospel is not being preached to the millions of unbelievers all around us.

A case in point. It is probably safe to say that few Christians today have read much about the English Civil War in the mid-seventeenth century. It is an eye-opening study. Rather than the typical wars about land, money and politics, this was essentially a war between various Protestant denominations, such as the Puritans and the Presbyterians, over doctrinal issues. It is shocking to read about huge bloody battles between brothers in Christ. And yet, though without cannons and swords, we continue to battle each other today.

Jesus tells us, "Blessed are the peacemakers, for they will be called sons of God" (Matthew 5:9). Can we fellowship with other Christians on "the other side" (whom we assume are in error) without acrimony? A line from the poet Longfellow may be appropriate: "The little I have seen in the world teaches me to look upon the errors of others in sorrow, not in anger."

You, the reader, are probably on one side or the other of the charismatic question. I urge you to worship God, in your own way, with all your might, without condemning others. Yes, we all know that excesses have been committed by extremists on both sides. Perhaps you have been offended by those in the other camp. Well, the Bible assures us that "a man's wisdom gives him patience; it is to his glory to overlook an offense" (Proverbs 19:11).

The Bible promises us that "peacemakers who sow in peace raise a harvest of righteousness" (James 3:18). What good can come of looking at the "speck . . . in your brother's eye" (Matthew 7:3)? The Holy Spirit, through Paul, insisted, "I want men everywhere to lift up holy hands in prayer, *without anger or disputing* (1 Timothy 2:8, emphasis added). (You don't really have to lift up your hands!)

Can We Learn from One Another?

If your heart's desire is to Worship God, and to Worship Him with greater potency and intimacy, then you will welcome help from any quarter within Christianity. It may come from the practices of churches you have never attended—or never want to attend. But if it will assist you in Worshiping the Lord, I hope you will open yourself up to some new ideas.

After observing the worship practices of a great variety of Christian churches, I have come to the conclusion that we would all do well to learn from each other. Different denominations seem to have some aspects of worship "perfected" more than others. Some churches are "high church," with an emphasis on liturgy and ceremony. Some are "low church," with scenes of strong emotional expression. Others are anywhere in between. Surely, in the Kingdom of God, there is room for all of us.

Listed below are a few suggestions for those of us who want to learn from one another. They contain generalizations, to be sure, but they can still help us. Please do not be offended if you feel that your "side" has been misrepresented. These are merely given as recommendations to hone our Worship skills, not to disparage any church or denomination.

What Charismatics Can Learn from Non-Charismatics About Worship

Surely one of the greatest strengths of many non-charismatic churches is their emphasis on the Bible in worship. (Yes, I know that charismatic churches also use the Bible, but none of us can ever use it enough!) The Scriptures take on a number of different aspects in corporate worship services, but can also help us in our private Worship.

Praying with Scripture

There are dozens of powerful prayers in the Word of God. These are not meant only for the person who prayed them many centuries ago but for believers of all epochs. It is wonderful to substitute the names of our loved ones in these great prayers, or any others in need of the Lord's grace. These biblical prayers form a model for all our praying and help assure that all our intercessions are in accordance with the Lord's will. E. M. Bounds, in his classic *The Necessity of Prayer*, states: "So to those who thus pray, the Bible becomes a new Bible, and Christ a new Savior, by the light and the revelation of the inner chamber."

Meditating on Scripture

God promised Joshua success if he would "meditate on [the Word] day and night" (Joshua 1:8). With the deplorable rise in transcendental meditation and other Eastern influences, many Christian churches have unfortunately avoided the entire topic of meditation. Yet God's Word does not change, and we are repeatedly admonished to meditate on the Scriptures. This is not for the purpose of making us renowned Bible scholars, but to help us know and Worship the author of the Book.

170

Memorizing the Word

Some of you may be objecting, "I thought we were learning how to Worship without any externals, including even a Bible." You are correct. I strongly recommend both praying Scriptures and meditating on the Word *without* having the Book physically before us. This means taking the time beforehand to memorize the Scriptures, as Peter admonishes us: "I want you to recall the words spoken in the past by the holy prophets and the command given by our Lord and Savior through your apostles" (2 Peter 3:2).

First of all, unless you are a brand-new believer, you *already* know more Scripture than you probably realize. Furthermore, it is good to memorize at least a verse or two each week. Some do well at learning whole chapters or books. Others like to memorize sets of verses arranged in topics, such as are found in the excellent "Topical Memory System" developed by the Navigator's ministry. Whichever you choose, remember that the more Scripture we store inside us—hiding it in our hearts (see Psalm 119:11)—the more we can use in our times of private Worship.

What Non-Charismatics Can Learn from Charismatics About Worship

For those non-charismatics who might be entering this section fearfully, you can relax. I am not suggesting that you burst out in tongues! But as we observed earlier, we can learn from other aspects of worship that are generally associated with the charismatic renewal—but that few Christians could find doctrinally offensive.

Speaking Expressions of Praise

King David claimed that "his praise will always be on my lips" (Psalm 34:1). Is this simply hyperbole? Not at all. Our reaction to something good (or perhaps even more so, to something bad) might be a verbal: "Praise God!" A reverent, worshipful string of biblical phrases should ever be cleansing our tongues: "Thank

You, Lord. Praise Your name, O Lord. I love You, Jesus." I do not mean an obnoxious parroting of unthinking verbiage, but a continuous flow of the recognition of God's presence. As Brother Lawrence encouraged those around him, we, too, should "form the habit of conversing all the time with God."

Motions of the Body

No, you do not have to be a ballerina to Worship God. But, can you lift your hands? Can you kneel down? Can you praise the Lord with the body He has given you? Can we follow David's example, as he exclaims, "I will praise you as long as I live, and in your name I will lift up my hands" (Psalm 63:4). Many people are very intimidated to be overt in corporate worship, but this can be liberating in times of private Worship. Such spirited praise declares to your very being that you are truly alone with God—without fear (or even thought) of men.

Waiting on God

This is an area of Worship in which almost all of us need more help. How often have we prayed for God's guidance and never given Him time to answer! Most of us are so time-pressure oriented that simply to "wait on God" seems rather a waste of time. Yet the biblical model is ever before us: "In the morning, O LORD, you hear my voice; in the morning I lay my requests before you *and wait in expectation*" (Psalm 5:3, emphasis added). It is in such moments that the Lord can speak peace to our souls. Whatever your personal beliefs about God's methods of divine guidance, all of us need to spend more time waiting on the Lord.

Where Do We Go from Here?

In the introduction to this book, I stated that its purpose was to bring the reader closer to Christ. It is now time to begin putting all the aspects we have discussed about Worship into a framework that we can use to change our lives.

The Scripture commands us to "clothe yourselves with the Lord Jesus Christ" (Romans 13:14). Like shopping for a new garment, we have looked at worship from a variety of viewpoints. Now we must "try it on" and, finding the right fit for us, begin to wear it on a daily basis.

This is the design of the final two chapters. In chapter nine, we put into practice the art of private Worship in its most elemental role—that of a quiet time alone with God. We will see that Worship itself—not praying, not Bible reading—should form an integral part of this fundamental Christian practice.

In the final chapter, we will go beyond our quiet time to find ways of embracing Worship throughout the day—in our everyday lifestyles. It is more than just a "life-changing experience." It is the very reason we were born.

chapter nine

Worship in Your Quiet Time

I will sing to the LORD all my life; I will sing praise to my
God as long as I live. May my meditation be pleasing to
him, as I rejoice in the LORD.

Psalm 104:33–34

Each day I will bless you, and I will praise your name forever and ever.

Greek Morning Hymn (second or third century)

These last two chapters contain the practical application of all we have considered in the previous pages of this book. All that we have learned—about worship, spending time with the Lord, music, God-consciousness, relationship—is now viewed in practical steps for our everyday lives. The previous eight chapters were a series of step-like introductory preludes to bring us to this point of implementation.

God created us to be worshipers, but that relationship was broken by the Fall and we must seek to restore it through a lifestyle of worship. This will mean a true focus on our Lord and a response to Him above all others.

To clearly mark the way of this journey of restoration, we will consider this "lifestyle of worship" in two ways:

1. improving the quality of Worship in our quiet times alone with God and
2. embarking on a continual state of Worship throughout our daily lives.

This chapter will cover the first way, the final chapter the second way.

Quiet Times Alone with God

This chapter assumes, of course, that the concept of having a daily quiet time is not a new one to us. Nevertheless, for those readers who may be unfamiliar with this invaluable practice, let's take a few moments to think about its importance. Of all the thousands (millions?) of activities you can experience, I submit that having a daily quiet time is the one that can have the greatest long-term effect on your Christian walk.

Granted, one can be a heaven-bound Christian without ever having a quiet time. One can even be a good churchgoer and a good Christian spouse or parent. Having a quiet time is assuredly not a requirement for salvation.

Yet if your desire is to know God more and to have a deeper relationship with Him, having a daily quiet time is unquestionably one of the best ways to go about it. In Jeremiah 24:7 God promises, "I will give them a heart to know me." As we saw in the first chapter of this book, the way you get to know someone is to spend time with him or her.

Jesus gives us a characterization of this relationship in the tenth chapter of John's gospel, concerning a shepherd and his sheep. He says, "His sheep follow him because they know his voice. But they will never follow a stranger; in fact, they will run away from him because they do not recognize a stranger's voice" (John 10:4–5). He then proclaims: "I am the good shepherd; I know my sheep and my sheep know me" (John 10:14). And He repeats: "My sheep listen to my voice; I know them, and they follow me" (John 10:27).

How does one get to know someone's voice? Does it happen quickly, or over a period of time? And who will get to know God's voice better: one who consistently spends time with Him or one who only does so when a crisis arises?

Many times individuals have come to me and asked for counsel about major decisions. I try to help, but ultimately they need to find direction from God. I generally ask, "Do you spend time with the Lord every day, getting to know His voice?" If the answer is negative, then we discuss how the needy Christian who does not know His voice could ever recognize the leading of the Lord when it comes.

Again, we are not to look at our quiet times as a means of *getting something*. We are not seeking the Lord to increase our knowledge or to make us better counselors. We Worship our Lord to be closer to Him. As Reformation theologian Johannes Eckhart stated, "If we seek God for our own good and profit, we are not seeking God."

The Key to Quality

If there is any one word that comes to mind about quality quiet times, it is *consistency*. The Christians who spend time with God "when they can find it" miss out on countless blessings from the Lord. Those who abandon this practice during times of spiritual drought often forfeit the very sustenance needed to survive the drought and break away from it. But those who persevere with a daily quiet time, even when they do not "feel like it," become servants who recognize their Master's voice and know the joy of intimate relationship with the God of the universe.

The Bible is replete with encouragement about this consistency. In Acts 17:11, the Bereans were commended because they "examined the Scriptures *every day*" (emphasis added). The believers after the resurrection "*stayed continually* at the temple, praising God" (Luke 24:53, emphasis added). Paul admonishes us to "be joyful *always;* pray *continually*" (1 Thessalonians 5:16–17, emphasis added). In the book of Hebrews, we find this command: "Through Jesus, therefore, let us *continually* offer to God a sacrifice of praise—the fruit of lips that confess his name" (Hebrews 13:15, emphasis added). The Old Testament is likewise teeming with "examples" and "exhortations" to worship daily.

Nevertheless, if you are new to this idea, please do not begin to worry about finding another hour every day! The length of one's quiet time is unique to each of us. Many of us would love to spend an hour each day alone with God, but it is not at all workable. No guilt trips are applicable concerning the length of your quiet time. Again, the key is consistency: It is far better to spend a little time every day than one long time once a week.

Any experienced music teacher can tell whether her students have practiced all week or crammed the night before the lesson after a week of neglect. It is better to practice thirty minutes each day than to have a marathon eight-hour practice session before a lesson. The way to improve as a musician is to spend time alone practicing every day, and the way to improve as a Christian is to spend time alone with God every day.

Adding to Your "Repertoire"

As Artistic Director of the MasterWorks Festival, I have the responsibility of hiring soloists to play concertos with our orchestra. (A concerto is a piece of music written for orchestra and a soloist. An example is a violin concerto—for violin soloist and orchestra.) Once a soloist is selected, there is still the question of which concerto he or she will play. Therefore, in the discussions with the soloist I will usually ask, "What is in your repertoire?"

The question means, "Of all the great concertos written for your instrument, which ones do you already know well and have ready to perform?" Let us suppose I am asking this of a piano soloist. He will respond with something like, "Well, I know all of the five Beethovens, the two Brahms, the Schumann, the Grieg, the Tchaikovsky, the first two Rachmaninoffs and the first Prokofiev." Then we will select one and program it for a performance at the Festival.

A top soloist will constantly be learning new pieces, thus adding them to his repertoire. The more pieces he knows, the more useful he will be as a soloist and the more performances he will be offered. Furthermore, he will regularly practice all the works in his repertoire, keeping them ready for performance. Adding new repertoire can never mean that you neglect those works you already know. All this, of course, is a Herculean effort. But it is part of being a world-class musician.

Let us take this analogy and apply it to our quiet times. What is in *your* repertoire? That is, what do you do in your quiet times that is effective? What do you do that regularly brings you closer to Christ and best equips you for His service?

For most of us, the answer is in two categories: prayer and Bible reading. And of course, these are two of the most meaningful things in the world that we can do! Every Christian is called to pray and to read God's Word. Furthermore, each of these two pillars of our quiet time has many subcategories: intercession, petition, various types of Bible study and so on.

179

Like a great musician, we need to be practicing these regularly while adding to our repertoire. The Scriptures admonish the wise to "add to their learning" (Proverbs 1:5). This chapter is about taking the two pillars of prayer and the Bible, and adding a new pillar: Worship. Like the other two pillars, it contains a number of marvelous subcategories to explore.

The Quiet Time Repertoire: The Bible

Before adding the new pillar of Worship, it is advisable to consider what we are already doing in the realms of Bible study and prayer. Obviously, this is not a book specifically about these subjects, yet they are so related to Worship that they should not be ignored. Furthermore, as we will see, some of the most effective parts of our quiet times can be when these various categories are used in combination.

Therefore, we will begin with God's Word. Its power to change lives has been testified to throughout many centuries by people from every segment of life. English writer Charles Dickens stated categorically: "The New Testament is the best book the world has ever known or will know." The famous Hollywood director Cecil B. DeMille once remarked: "After more than sixty years of almost daily reading in the Bible, I never fail to find it always new and marvelously in tune with the changing needs of every day."

How do you use the Bible in your quiet times? Let us consider different ways it may be read devotionally. Many people have found great delight in

- Reading it cover to cover. (Start in Genesis and finish in Revelation, reading one or more chapters each day, then begin again.)
- Reading the Old and New Testaments simultaneously. (Start in Genesis, in Psalms and in Matthew, reading one chapter from each grouping each day, and read to the end

of each grouping. It does not quite work out evenly, but you can be flexible.)

- Endless variations on the above. (For example: Start at Genesis, Psalms, Isaiah, Matthew and Romans, reading five chapters each day. Again, flexibility will be needed to make it come out together.)
- Reading along with a daily guide. (Dozens of these are available, both in print and on the Internet, from many Christian ministries and churches.)
- Reading randomly. (Although this horrifies some Bible scholars, many people simply open the Bible randomly every day and begin reading.)
- Reading from different translations. (Unless you know Greek and Hebrew and can study the original, it can be helpful to compare various translations to bring out different facets of the Word.)

What about Bible study? Suppose you want to dig deeper into the truths of the Word each day. Again, there are many excellent courses open to you. A few favorites include:

- topical Bible study
- biographical Bible study
- "character quality" Bible study
- thematic Bible study
- word study
- chapter summary
- book survey
- combinations and variations of the above methods

What about *memorizing* God's Word? This will be extremely helpful for the topic of the final chapter: Worship as a lifestyle. How can one "meditate . . . day and night" (Joshua 1:8) on the Scriptures unless one has first "hidden" His Word in one's heart (see Psalm 119:11)?

181

Storing the Word within our memories increases our understanding of it. As the great German writer Goethe reminds us, "The Bible grows more beautiful as we grow in our understanding of it." This is why the book of Proverbs refers to Scripture with the following admonishment: "It is pleasing when you keep [the sayings of the wise] in your heart and have all of them ready on your lips" (Proverbs 22:18).

The two basic styles of Scripture memory methods are:

1. Memorizing single verses that are usually grouped in specific topics. (Some topics are God's promises, our love for one another, humility. You can select the verses yourself, or purchase guidance materials from ministries like the Navigators.)
2. Memorizing complete chapters or books. (This wonderful practice may seem overwhelming at first, but it is simply a matter of learning a few verses each week for an extended period of time. The old adage "How do you eat an elephant? One bite at a time" could be paraphrased "How do you memorize the Sermon on the Mount? One verse at a time.")

Some people memorize Scripture by repeating it over and over orally. Some people write the verses down. Others listen to tape recordings of the Bible being read. Whatever method is used, victory is usually given to those who are slow and steady (consistent!) rather than those who excitedly try to memorize a chapter in a week—only to give up in disappointment and never try again.

The Quiet Time Repertoire: Prayer

As with our study of the Bible, the topic of prayer is broad enough to fill the space of many voluminous books. The poet Coleridge describes prayer as "the very highest energy of which the mind is capable." The following paragraphs are given to help those of us who tend to think of prayer as simply *asking* God for things. As we expand our prayer lives, we will be more effective in combining prayer with Worshiping our Lord.

Thanksgiving

Perhaps our greatest sin of omission is that of ingratitude. We need consciously to thank God every day for His goodness to us: for our salvation, our health, our abilities, our loved ones, our friends, our church, our provision . . . and for a thousand other blessings.

Contrition

Very often we admit that "we are sinners saved by grace." But how often do we take time to confess our sins to God and ask for forgiveness? In order to Worship the Lord, we need to be clean before Him, keeping "short accounts" with Him, acknowledging our sins and being washed white as snow before God.

Dedication

Being born again is not the end of it; we need to dedicate ourselves anew to the Lord each day. Furthermore, we should dedicate all that we are doing to God and to His glory. This covers not only our occupations and particular tasks for the day, but also our thought lives, our deliberations and judgments.

Intercession

Not only does God invite us to ask Him to meet our needs, He desires, of course, that we also pray on behalf of others. This incredible gift can be used for every individual on earth—not only family and friends, but complete strangers, those in authority and even our enemies.

Relinquishment

In all our prayers, there is a place for saying "Thy will be done." For example, we may desire a new job but must be willing to remain where we are if it is the Lord's will.

No matter what the price, we must relinquish our "rights" to God and pray for His contentment to be upon us in every circumstance.

Spiritual Warfare

There is a spiritual enemy to all our prayers, and God has given us the authority to bind, rebuke and constrain him and his evil activities against us. The subject of spiritual warfare is a difficult one for most of us to comprehend clearly, but it cannot be ignored. We should ask God to protect us from any satanic interference in our lives and our thoughts of Worship.

The Quiet Time Repertoire: Worship

American President Calvin Coolidge once remarked, "It is only when men begin to worship that men begin to grow." It is now time for *us* to grow, and to add to our repertoire. Let us put our pens and paper (and even our Bibles) aside and focus entirely on the Lord. Some of these ideas for Worshiping God have been mentioned before in this book and some may be completely new to you. Remember: It is not so important to do everything suggested here, but we do want to expand our repertoires in order to Worship the Lord with everything we have.

Speaking Praise to God

"My mouth is filled with your praise, declaring your splendor all day long" (Psalm 71:8). In your own words

- tell the Lord you love Him, and why you love Him
- thank Him for His faithfulness

- declare that He is worthy of praise and glory
- list His many attributes: "You are loving; You are steadfast"
- shout "Hallelujah!" and other words of praise and exaltation
- speak of the many ways in which He has blessed you
- confess to God your gratefulness to be His child
- personalize Scriptures that come to mind: "Let everything that is within me praise Your holy name!"

Singing Songs to God

"Sing and make music in your heart to the Lord" (Ephesians 5:19). Add to your words the melody of a song of praise. Ask the Lord to bring a song to mind that expresses your love for Him. It does not matter whether the song be old or new; what matters is that it unleashes praise from your heart. Concentrate on truly *meaning* the words you are singing, and stay focused on the Lord.

Singing Spontaneous Praise to God

"Sing to the LORD a new song" (Psalm 96:1). Continue to sing, but begin adding your own words of praise—even if they are simply a repetition of the same phrases. As you gain confidence, make up your own melodies as well as your own words. Do not worry about the musical quality of such improvising; concentrate on singing praise to God. To our God—who created the universe and is *far* above all earthly standards of music— it will sound more beautiful than the most exquisite Mozart arias.

Physical Activity

"Come, let us bow down in worship, let us kneel before the LORD our maker" (Psalm 95:6). We are not part of God's "frozen chosen." Lift up your hands to God. Or kneel before Him. Or bow down in reverence. Perhaps you will feel led to walk about, praising the Lord with every part of you. He created our bodies; He is not embarrassed by them as we sometimes are. Ask Him to lead you and encourage you in this biblical area of Worship.

Adoration

"Be still, and know that I am God" (Psalm 46:10). There are also times to be quiet before the Lord in awe-inspired adoration. This is when we bask in the presence of God as a sunbather soaks up the rays of the sun. No words, music or motions are usually needed. As David did, simply "[sit] before the LORD" (2 Samuel 7:18) and feel the joy of His closeness to you.

Communion with God

"And he said to them, 'I have eagerly desired to eat this Passover with you . . .'" (Luke 22:15). Many of us think of the word *communion* as something formal or liturgical. But it really means "to commune" with the Lord, that is, *to do normal things together with Him.* Eating—"breaking bread"—is only one example. Many take a "worship walk" with the Lord.

Others do certain tasks—draw, write, sketch—as a worshipful time of communion with God. The important point is to be fully aware of the Lord's presence and guiding direction.

Meditating on the Word

"Oh, how I love your law! I meditate on it all day long!" (Psalm 119:97). The word *meditate* should not conjure up scenes of an Eastern guru chanting, "Oooommm." God told Joshua to meditate on "this Book of the Law" day and night (Joshua 1:8). The word *meditate* means "to ponder, to contemplate, to cogitate, to ruminate, to mull over, to reflect upon, to think about." It means to apply these verbs to a line of Scripture, asking God to reveal Himself through this biblical meditation.

Waiting on God

"Wait for the LORD; be strong and take heart and wait for the LORD" (Psalm 27:14). A key part of Worship is waiting on God. This is different from adoration in that waiting assumes a completely passive state. It is a time of seeking the Lord's guidance and should be exercised generally after a time of prayer. Once you have cleansed yourself of sin and have established a dedicated attitude of communion with God, stop and wait. Do nothing. But stay in a posture of Worship and wait to see if God directs you in any way. Remember the words of the great Christian writer Andrew Murray: "Listening to God's voice is the secret of the assurance that he will listen to mine."

Keeping Our Balance

Do not be dismayed by the long list of new things to attempt in your quiet times! You do not have to try them all at once! Remember the analogy of the concerto soloists. They are always adding new pieces to their repertoire, but they add them *one piece at a time*.

Proverbs 13:11 gives us an important principle about adding to a repertoire. It is given in the context of money, but the principle works for any asset we want to acquire. The verse states: "He who gathers money *little by little* makes it grow" (Proverbs 13:11). The surest way to add to a pocketbook, a store of knowledge or a Worship repertoire is little by little—not in erratic leaps and bounds.

Furthermore, we learn best by association, with the lessons placed in the proper order. One does not start a young child with trigonometry! But step-by-step—through arithmetic, algebra, geometry—the student is progressively taught the stages of knowledge that will eventually enable him or her to master trigonometry.

Therefore, a good plan in adding Worship to your quiet times is a progressive one. Prayerfully select one of the items listed above, preferably one that is not too alien to your personality and past practices. (If you are a quiet person, you do not have to start by shouting "Hallelujah!")

Add your selection into tomorrow's quiet time. It may seem odd at first, but persevere. Practice it for at least a week before adding another. Then select another to add to your quiet time for a while, and so on. Do not succumb to hurrying the process; we have the rest of our lives (and all of eternity) to Worship. Better to add things "little by little" and have them last than try too much, become overwhelmed and lose them all.

A warning: As with any other discipline, adding Worship to your quiet time will not be easy. It requires additional time and effort, and though "the spirit is willing, . . . the body is weak" (Mark 14:38). The devil will also try everything to deter regular Worship. Success will not happen without faith and determination. If this duty seems daunting, remember the words of Scottish writer George MacDonald: "The doing of things from duty is but a stage on the road to the kingdom of truth and love." Ultimately, whatever efforts we make will be a small price to pay for such a life-changing custom.

A Few Basics to Consider

As you add new items into your quiet time, remember the basic concept, which can be summed up in three points:

1. We should add Worship—of some variety—to our daily quiet times.
2. We should develop a broad repertoire in all three categories from which to select.
3. We should endeavor to find a balance in Worship, prayer and Bible reading, as well as finding a balance in the categories under each list.

Our creative God does not want each of us to be crammed into some mold, all doing the exact same things in our times alone with Him. He created our different personalities and loves each of them. Therefore, we can each find our unique balance from a wide repertoire when we have our quiet times. Here are three topics to help you find your own balance.

Where?

Let us clarify at the beginning that an effective quiet time can take place anywhere. Christians have worshiped God in slums, prisons, catacombs and concentration camps. David asserted, "If I make my bed in the depths [Sheol], you are there" (Psalm 139:8). And David would have worshiped the Lord while he was there, you can be sure!

We see that we can Worship the Lord anywhere, but by the same token there is no valor in purposely seeking out a wretched place for our quiet times. On the contrary, we should seek a place of beauty, serenity and inspiration whenever possible. As the poet Longfellow recalls for us, "We lead but one life here on earth. We must make that beautiful."

Most of all, we should have our quiet times in places with as few distractions as possible. For many of us, this can be quite a challenge. Privacy can be hard to come by! If your quiet time is to be inside, use Jesus' admonition to "go into your room, close the door and pray" (Matthew 6:6). In this situation, it is best to choose a room with the greatest beauty and order possible. This can be either the beauty of nature (by way of windows to the outdoors) or the man-made beauty of visual art and orderliness.

As I mentioned previously, an ideal place for some of us is to be outdoors when possible. (Obviously, inclement weather affects your choice.) If you live in the city, perhaps you can find a park or an open space that can remind you of the beauty of God's nature. Again, finding a *remote* place is imperative, where you are the least likely to be distracted, interrupted or inhibited in any way.

Still another possibility—especially if the weather is bad and no privacy can be found in your house—is to seek out another indoor situation. I have had quiet times in empty church buildings and in my parked car, in libraries and in art galleries. (In these latter two locations privacy is rather lessened, so you had better not try singing!) The basic principles remain the same: Go where you can be alone with God. If aspects of beauty and order can be nearby, all the better.

When?

One question that can be rather contentious among believers is: *When?* That is, when is the best time of the day to have a quiet time with God? Many Christians insist that the beginning of the day is the most opportune time, the sentiment expressed well by John Bunyan: "He who runs from God in the morning will scarcely find him the rest of the day." There are a number of Scriptures about "seeking Him early," such as Psalm 119:147: "I rise before dawn and cry for help; I have put my hope in your word." Yet the very next verse says: "My eyes stay open through the watches of the night, that I may meditate on your promises" (verse 148). Certainly many believers have effectual quiet times late at night.

And there are, of course, seasons in one's life when having a quiet time at any point of day or night is terribly difficult. This is notably true for mothers of small children or caretakers of people with special needs. If this describes you, here are two points to remember. First, no guilt trips! God understands that sometimes it is impossible for a proper quiet time. He knows your heart and realizes that your life will not always be this hectic. And, second, do what you can, even in snatches. Susanna Wesley—the mother of many children (including the renowned John and Charles Wesley)—had her quiet time by sitting in the middle of the floor with her apron pulled over her head! (Her children learned that when Mother is in this posture, she is "not on duty.")

Rather than insist on a legalistic standard, perhaps it is best if each of us finds the best time for our unique circumstances and personalities. This can be guided by two basic principles:

1. It should be at a time when we are *at our best*. Like the blemished animal sacrifices condemned in the Old Testament, we would not want to appear before the Lord in our

ebb point. Are you a morning person? Then have your quiet times in the morning. Are you a night person? Then offer your best to God every night.

2. We should aim for consistency, both in place and time. This does not mean a rigid ritual, year in and year out. It is generally easier, though, to form a habit if not too many variables are involved. If you feel in a rut, a measure of change might be helpful. But a rut will never occur unless a habit is long established in our lives.

How?

Another important question: Is there a particular order to follow? In a word, no. Some will want to pray first, then study the Word, then have a time of Worship. Others will Worship first, then pray, then open the Bible. And then there are numerous combinations of the different elements within each of these categories. God is glorified in all of them. Some books insist on following a certain order (such as, "You need to 'enter His gates with praise'") but such instructions are taken from *interpretations* of Scripture. The Bible itself does not give any such restrictions about our quiet times; perhaps this is because God wants each of us to seek Him for direction in this very personal area.

You might want to put the area that is the most difficult for you *first*, to make certain it will not be under-emphasized or ignored. Some of us are great prayer warriors, but weak on Worship and Bible reading. Then put Worship and the Bible first. Unless you start with the difficult parts, you may tend to rush through them at the end.

Now let's put this together into samples that might be of help to you as you develop Worship in your quiet times.

Some Examples: An Ideal Quiet Time

For the sake of those readers who are new to this, I will give details for a few "sample quiet times." These are *not* to be fol-

191

lowed ritualistically; they are only for purposes of clarification. I hope that they will stir your own imagination to see the multitudinous possibilities and inspire you to seek the Lord for His direction in your unique quiet times.

Example One: A Short Quiet Time (5–10 Minutes)

1. *Bible:* Read two chapters of Scripture (3–5 minutes).
2. *Prayer:* Intercede for those in your immediate family (2–3 minutes).
3. *Worship:* Spend time singing spontaneous praise (1–2 minutes).

Example Two: A Moderate Quiet Time (15–20 Minutes)

1. *Prayer:* Ask God's forgiveness for specific sins (2–3 minutes).
2. *Worship:* Speak praise to God (1–2 minutes).
3. *Bible:* Work on a "character quality" Bible study (7–8 minutes).
4. *Worship:* Meditate on a verse of Scripture that comes to mind (3–4 minutes).
5. *Prayer:* Thank the Lord for His many blessings (2–3 minutes).

Example Three: An Extended Quiet Time (One Hour, Approximately)

1. *Worship:* Sing several songs of praise (3–5 minutes).
2. *Bible:* Read five chapters of Scripture (10–12 minutes).
3. *Prayer:* Dedicate yourself and your Bible study to God (2–3 minutes).
4. *Bible:* Study the life and writings of Peter (15–20 minutes).
5. *Worship:* Take a "worship walk" with God, speaking praise (7–10 minutes).

6. *Prayer:* Intercede for your loved ones and the needs of your community (2–3 minutes).
7. *Bible:* Freely search the Scriptures, asking God to speak through them (5–8 minutes).
8. *Prayer:* Lay your burdens and needs before the Lord (5–8 minutes).
9. *Worship:* Spend several moments waiting on God for guidance (3–5 minutes).

The noted French writer Balzac rightly tells us that "for the Christian who loves God, worship is the daily bread of patience." If we are patient to take the time we should for Worship, then we discover the absolute joy of knowing the Lord's presence in our lives on this earth—long before we know His presence for eternity in heaven.

I hope that the above examples are helpful to you. If not, forget about them and ask God to show you what should be a part of *your* daily quiet time. Remember, though, that the inclusion of Worship is essential and will help prepare you for the supreme worship experience we find in the final chapter: that of the abiding lifestyle of the inveterate worshiper.

Now is the time to take what we have been given in our quiet times and have it spill over into our entire lives. For as English poet John Donne pointed out, regarding the importance of connecting our quiet times and our lifestyles: "Of all commentaries on the Scriptures, *good examples* are the best and the liveliest."

chapter ten

Worship as a Lifestyle

Through Jesus, therefore, let us continually offer to God a sacrifice of praise—the fruit of lips that confess his name.

Hebrews 13:15

Let us give our thoughts completely to knowing God. The more one knows him, the more one wants to know him.

Brother Lawrence

There is an old adage that has many variations, but the central truth is clear: "When you sow a thought, you reap an action; when you sow an action, you reap a habit; when you sow a habit, you reap a character; when you sow a character, you reap a lifestyle."

What we call our lifestyles are really a vast collection of our thoughts, actions and habits, guided by our character. In this respect, we must admit that our lifestyles are ultimately up to us. The Lord has given us stewardship over these areas and expects us to cultivate our lives as a good farmer cultivates a field: that it may bring forth a great harvest for God's glory.

If we are unhappy about our lifestyles, we cannot blame it on anyone else—or on society, or our upbringings, or our environments. We must change our thoughts, actions and habits. As the great poet Dryden notes: "We first make our habits, then our habits make us."

Let us define the words of the famous adage written above from the point of view of this book:

> *Thought:* God-consciousness. We become aware of God and want to respond to Him.
> *Action:* our immediate response. We pray, Worship Him or read the Bible.
> *Habit:* quiet time. We turn these actions into a daily part of our lives.
> *Character:* Christian character. Our hearts are changed by God's abiding influence.
> *Lifestyle:* a lifestyle of worship. We consciously live our lives in God's presence.

In the preceding chapter, we looked at the importance of adding Worship to our daily quiet times. Now we will expand this concept, finding ways to embrace Worship throughout the day in all of our "mundane" activities—that is, in every part of our lives. Paul admonishes us: "Be very careful, then, how you live—not as unwise but as wise, making the most of every opportunity, because the days are evil" (Ephesians 5:15–16).

As we will see, there are no mundane activities when they are done to glorify the Lord. Cleaning a bathroom while Worshiping God is far more "spiritual" than preaching a sermon while being unaware of His divine presence. Brother Lawrence expressed it in this way: "We should apply ourselves continually, so that, without exception, all our actions become small occasions of fellowship with God, yet artlessly, but just as it arises from the purity and the simplicity of the heart."

The Practice of the Presence of God

Let us consider this obscure man named Nicholas Herman, who entered a monastery in the middle of the seventeenth century and became known as Brother Lawrence. He never rose to fame or prominence, but those who knew him always remembered his joy, his peaceful countenance and his inspiring devotion to the Lord. To use Brother Lawrence's own words, he "practiced the presence of God" in all his daily activities.

He was not a preacher or a church leader. In fact, most of his life in the monastery seems to have been spent scrubbing pans in the kitchen or doing other tiresome chores. It made little difference to him. He once explained, "I turn my little omelette in the pan for the love of God. When it is finished if I have nothing to do, I prostrate myself on the ground and worship my God—who gave me the grace to make it—after which I am happier than a king. When I can do nothing else, it is enough to have picked up a straw for the love of God."

Although Brother Lawrence did not consider himself a teacher or writer, those around him prevailed upon him to write down the spiritual principles on which he based his exceedingly devoted life. In his short *Practices Essential to Acquire the Spiritual Life*, he defines the practice of the presence of God—"that is to find joy in his divine company and to make it a habit of life, speaking humbly and conversing lovingly with him at all times—every moment, without rule or restriction."

Of course, today we read this with admiration, but a part of us objects: "That's fine for Brother Lawrence in a seventeenth-century monastery. But what about me? How does this relate to my life today? How well would Brother Lawrence have done if he had had my high-pressure job, my crabby boss, my demanding family and my stressful lifestyle?"

Good questions. I, too, wonder how well Brother Lawrence would have practiced the presence of God in a twenty-first-century American metropolis. When I look at the absurdly busy life I presently lead, a little time in a monastery sounds rather nice. Perhaps you feel the same way.

Nevertheless, I believe that this uncelebrated man who died in 1691 discovered a profound (and often overlooked) key about the Christian walk that can be applied to our own lives. We will need to "translate" the seventeenth-century words and environment to fit our modern circumstances, but it is worth the effort. In this final chapter we will quote quite a bit from Brother Lawrence as we seek to Worship God in our everyday activities as he did.

Twenty-First-Century Lifestyles

When we study today's fast-paced lives from a historical point of view, we find two primary differences between the lifestyle of the twenty-first century and that of the seventeenth—or for that matter the twelfth or fourth. The two critical differences are these:

First, we cram much more activity into our lives today. The last century's many "labor-saving" inventions have given us more leisure time, but the "pleasure-giving" inventions have beguiled us into choking these leisure times with a mania of busyness. In other words, when we have an extra hour, we tend to cram three hours of activity into it. It reminds us of the alarming conclusion drawn by Emerson: "We have become the tools of our tools."

Before the invention of the light bulb—a relatively modern invention within the last twenty centuries of Christianity—most people went to bed soon after the sun went down. What an amazing idea this seems to us today! Since the advent of recorded sound and mass media—radio, television, 24-hour news, the Internet—our hours are filled with endless possibilities that reduce us to mere spectators. The automobile was invented to save us time, but it hardly seems so when we are sitting in rush-hour traffic. The computer, too, was built to save us time; but after several hours of surfing the Net, one begins to wonder.

Second, we have much more control over our personal activities today. This may surprise or even shock you, but it is true. The freedoms that we take for granted today have been rare throughout history (and are not universal even today). You may say that you hate your job and it works you too hard. Well, you could quit it and find work elsewhere—and no government, king, overlord or slave master will prevent you. This is a wonderful and very modern *luxury!*

We can choose our careers, our education, our jobs, our spouses, even where we live. A few centuries ago this would have been impossible for all but the top echelons of society. Furthermore, our jobs give us much more leisure time than the six-day-a-week, ten-hour-a-day jobs of the nineteenth century. As for farmers (who were one half of all American workers until 1860), they woke at dawn, worked until sunset and went to bed. This had been going on for centuries. Not a lot of leisure time.

By reversing these two points, one might say that (1) the good news is that we have much more freedom of choice in how we spend our time today and (2) the bad news is that we often make very stupid (and very busy) choices in how we spend our time.

How we need to cry out to God, like Moses in Psalm 90: "Teach us to number our days aright, that we may gain a heart of wisdom" (Psalm 90:12)!

Finding the Time

With all this as a backdrop, now consider your personal lifestyle. Of course, every reader will have a different situation, but I must assume that if you bought this book, then you truly desire to spend more time Worshiping God than you are presently doing. Now, each of us has exactly 24 hours each day. So, for you to *add* any new activity (such as Worshiping God) will mean, of course, that you will first have to *subtract* some other activity in which you are presently involved.

Don't panic! I do not mean that you have to quit your various clubs, throw out any hobbies and kick in the television. (God may or may not be telling you to do so at times, but I am not.) We need a degree of rest, relaxation and recreation, and there is no need to feel guilty about it. How you spend your relaxation and recreation time is your own business. Certainly we each should check ourselves from time to time in order to re-evaluate our priorities. But this book is not for that purpose.

No, this book is to help you Worship God more in your *present* lifestyle. But as was mentioned above, we cannot add without subtracting. What then shall be subtracted to make room for Worshiping the Lord?

The answer is, for lack of a better word, *vegetating*. That is, every day we waste a huge amount of time vegetating, when we could be Worshiping.

What is vegetating? Let me explain by asking a number of questions:

What were you thinking about when you showered yesterday?
What were you thinking about when you waited in the bank line yesterday?
What were you thinking about when you shaved yesterday?
What were you thinking about when you waited for your computer to start up yesterday?

Do you know the answer to any of these questions? Most of us haven't a clue. You may answer, "I suppose I was thinking something, but it wasn't that important and I can't remember what it was." Perhaps. But for most of us, the honest truth is that we were not really thinking about anything in particular at those times. We were "zoned out." We were wasting mental time. We were vegetating.

Is this such a horrible crime? Of course not. But it does represent a vast amount of time every day that could have been spent Worshiping the Lord. As Thoreau reminds us, "You cannot kill time without injuring eternity." Trying to spend less time vegetating is simply the price one must pay in order to spend more time consciously Worshiping.

Vegetating Versus Worshiping

You see, when many of us read about someone like Brother Lawrence we make a critical mistake. We think that he was able to practice the presence of God while scrubbing dishes because he was such a wonderful, holy person. In other words, we assume that he could do this because of some special ability or talent that *he* had but we do not. This is both a mistake and a cop-out—one that we use all too often to excuse our own lack of Worshiping.

The real reason Brother Lawrence was able to practice the presence of God while scrubbing dishes was that—instead of "zoning out" as most of us do while scrubbing dishes—he consciously Worshiped, prayed, sang and spoke praise (at least mentally) during those times of ordinary work. Instead of vegetating, he chose to Worship.

How much of our time could be spent like this? How many things do we do every day that take no real thinking? Things that are rather automatic? Some scientists have estimated that as much as 50 to 70 percent of one's day is spent this way. Most of our routine activities—unless they are directly involved with speaking, writing or communicating with someone—fall into this category. Whatever your lifestyle, we all indulge in unnecessary vegetating every day.

Most of us probably do not waste *large* amounts of time; it is in the small moments that we could improve. The great Christian teacher G. Campbell Morgan once exhorted those around him: "Let the year be given to God in its every moment! The year is made up of minutes: let these be watched as having been dedicated to God. It is in the sanctification of the small that hallowing of the large is secure."

Again, please understand that I am *not* talking about rest, relaxation or recreation. These are beneficial and necessary, and we should consciously choose them. Vegetating is neither beneficial nor necessary. It is not even something we consciously choose to do. It is a waste: Our bodies are busy but our minds are vacant, unoccupied, meaningless, blank.

All that time we could have been Worshiping the Lord.

Finding the Time

In the previous chapter I gave three examples of quiet times for the sake of illustration. These examples were not meant to be rigidly imitated, and neither is the one I offer below. It is given primarily to show that *any* time we have available can be used for Worship. It does not have to be in a church and you do not have to be in a "holy" mood. You simply decide to Worship the Lord.

As I type this on my laptop computer, I am alone in my car. Don't worry, I'm not driving down the highway! I am waiting in a line of vehicles at a service station. In our state (Virginia), each car has to pass an annual inspection and ours is due this week. I will probably be waiting for fifteen or twenty minutes.

Now I decide to turn off the computer and spend time Worshiping God.

- I begin with verbal praise: "I worship You, Lord, for You are worthy. You are worthy of praise and honor and glory.

Hallelujah! Thank You for Your goodness to me. Thank You for my family. Bless each of them today, Lord. Thank You for this time we have together." (This continues for a moment or so more.)

- Then I intercede for a number of people: for our president, for the Supreme Court members and other political leaders, for my pastor.
- Recalling a verse I read earlier this morning, I meditate on its truth: "Whoever gives heed to instruction prospers, and blessed is he who trusts in the LORD" (Proverbs 16:20).
- Finally, I sit quietly before the Lord, basking in His presence and the knowledge of His closeness to me.

As I notice that the car in front of me is about to move, I thank God for the Worship we have enjoyed together. Putting the car in gear, I am grateful for the precious time I have just had with the Creator of the universe. I believe He enjoyed it as well.

Now the computer is switched on and I type the above paragraphs, recounting the activities of my brief Worship time. It was so simple. It did not take a church or a minister or a choir or even a Bible. It only took a desire to Worship God.

Such a Worship service in my car reminds me once again of the words of Brother Lawrence: "It is not needful always to be in church to be with God. We can make a chapel of our heart, to which we can from time to time withdraw to have gentle, humble, loving communion with him."

Consider the alternatives—that is, the things I could have done while waiting in this line.

I could have

- thought about something that needed pondering
- listened to the radio
- listened to a tape or CD
- vegetated (I might have been doing this even while listening to the radio, tape or CD)

Let me repeat: There is nothing wrong or sinful with any of the above choices. (Well, I suppose that if I entertained *evil* thoughts while waiting in my car, I would have been sinning.) But that is not the point. We do not Worship the Lord only for the purpose of keeping us from sin.

We Worship the Lord because we love Him, because He is worthy of our praise, because we want to deepen our relationship with Him: "Come, let us bow down in worship, let us kneel before the LORD our Maker; for he is our God and we are the people of his pasture, the flock under his care" (Psalm 95:6–7).

How do we begin to harvest our wasted time and use it to Worship the Lord? Prayerfully you should ask God to show you those areas in life where you habitually vegetate. We need to internalize and make practical those things we have accepted in theory. American poet Edwin Markham once wrote: "We have committed the Golden Rule to memory. Let us now commit it to life." In the same way, we need to stop vegetating in order to take Worship and "commit it to life."

To give you a head start on this lifetime process, we will consider two broad categories in which vegetating can be easily replaced with Worshiping: the incredible amount of time we spend waiting and vegetating, and those things we do regularly in which we often vegetate.

Waiting and Vegetating

Suppose you decide that every time you turn on your computer, or wait for a website to appear, you spend a moment Worshiping God. For many of us who spend all day in front of computers, such a practice could revolutionize our lives.

How about the endless times you are placed on hold while on the telephone? Rather than brood over this wasted time, Worship the Lord! You will find yourself in a much better mood when someone finally begins talking to you.

How much of our time is spent waiting in lines? I have already mentioned my time today waiting in a line of cars for inspection, but what about waiting in traffic? Your attitude about traffic will change drastically with Worship. What about "people lines" in the grocery store, the bank, the department store? These are great times for momentary Worship.

On your next car trip alone, consider having "red light Worship." Every time the light changes from green to red and you have to stop, spend the time Worshiping the Lord. (But keep your eyes on the light or your Worship will soon be interrupted by car horns!)

This list could go on and on, but you get the idea. Examine your own life to find those times of waiting and vegetating that could be harvested for Worship. Remember that much of the work we do each day uses little mental energy and could be coupled with Worship. Bernard of Clairvaux suggested that "he who labors as he prays lifts his heart to God with his hands."

Vegetating in Our Regular Tasks

As we prepare for the day, we have a good deal of time that can include Worship. Showering, shaving, putting on makeup . . . all of these are necessary yet take little or no mental effort. The father of Hudson Taylor, the legendary missionary to China, taught his son to pray and worship each morning as he got dressed. He knew that this was a task that he would do thousands of times for the rest of his life. Good advice!

If you are driving in the car alone over the same routes, you can experience times of Worship without becoming an irresponsible driver. For example, there is a certain stretch of straight, deserted road near our home with practically no traffic or pedestrians. Every time I am on that road I have a short but rich time of Worship.

Speaking of traveling, what about *walking?* You may not take long, contemplative walks in the country, but you do walk from place to place all day. Can you use this time to Worship the Lord? I recently read of a Civil War general who, even in the stress of battle, would consciously Worship God every time he mounted his horse. He put away the thoughts and responsibility of war until the end of his travel.

205

Do you ever eat alone? This is a wonderful and appropriate time to Worship and praise God. We can thank Him for every bite and show our gratitude for this provision in inner praise.

Again our list could continue much further. Let us examine our individual lives with an eye for finding times that we are regularly alone—if even for a moment. All too often we make the mistake of Worshiping God only if we have an extended time, such as a proper quiet time. But a lifestyle of Worship uses as many as possible of the "cracks and crevices" of time throughout the day.

Do you remember the example given by Nehemiah of the "split-second prayer"? "The king said to me, 'What is it you want?' *Then I prayed to the God of heaven,* and I answered the king . . ." (Nehemiah 2:4–5). If we can petition the Lord in a moment of time, then we can also Worship Him in the short instances of our day.

Of course, this is different for every person, and for many of us it is a formidable challenge. Once I was told by an elementary school teacher, "The only time I have alone all day is at lunch and when I go to the bathroom." Perhaps your job is equally stressful. What can you do in such circumstances? The answer: "Worship God at lunch and when you go to the bathroom."

It is not the amount of time that pleases the Lord; it is the heart that desires to Worship Him whenever possible. French novelist Anatole France gave us a wonderful image: "The time God allots to each of us is like a precious tissue on which we embroider as we best know how." What better embroidery can there be than our Worship of the Lord?

Being Good Stewards of Our "Thought Lives"

Why is this so important? Why is the direction of our thoughts so vital to the Christian walk? Because what we are talking about, ultimately, is stewardship, the good and right use of what God has given us.

Now in Christian teaching today, we hear a great deal about stewardship. Unfortunately, this excellent teaching is often limited to the areas of finance and giving. While these are important, they are also perhaps the easiest areas of our lives in which to practice good stewardship. In other words, it is possible to tithe or double-tithe our income and yet give very little *of ourselves* toward a relationship with God.

And some believers will add to the concept of financial stewardship the idea of being a good steward of our activities—working with the homeless, for instance, or teaching Sunday school. This, too, is undeniably an important part of our Christian walk—giving of our time and energy in service to the Lord. Obviously, how much time we give to the Lord will say a great deal about our relationship to Christ.

But stewardship involves more. It involves every part of ourselves—what we offer, what we do and, most importantly, what we think. Our thought lives are the ultimate stewardship, because our thoughts are known only by ourselves and God. How we spend our finances and activities we engage in are external; our thoughts are completely internal. They are the truest reflection of who we really are.

The expression "We become what we think about" is true. It comes directly from the King James Version of Proverbs 23:7, which states, "As [a man] thinketh in his heart, so is he." It is further founded upon the words of our Lord, who explained that "out of the overflow of the heart the mouth speaks" (Matthew 12:34). Our habitual thoughts fill up our hearts, and this will always control our words and actions. No wonder Paul insists that "we take captive every thought to make it obedient to Christ" (2 Corinthians 10:5).

This means that, as we Worship God and become more Christlike, our actual thoughts are relinquished to His leading. This is the ultimate and glorious surrender to God's Lordship, and it can have amazing consequences in our lives. This Christ-led thought life reminds me of the words of the illustrious astronomer Johannes Kepler. *During the mental tasks of studying astronomy,* he proclaimed to the Lord, "O God, I am thinking thy thoughts after thee."

Consider also a key passage given toward the end of the Sermon on the Mount: "Many will say to me on that day, 'Lord, Lord, did we not prophesy in your name, and in your name drive out demons and perform many miracles?' Then I will tell them plainly, *'I never knew you.* Away from me, you evildoers!'" (Matthew 7:22–23, emphasis added).

If there is one phrase I never want to hear from the Lord, it is "I never knew you." Since we know that He desires a close relationship with us, the only way these terrible words could ever be said to us is if we did not endeavor to mature in our relationship with Him. And much of this is accomplished through good stewardship of our thoughts toward Him.

No Guilt Please!

At this point, there may be some readers who are saying, "I just can't do it! I can't think about God constantly. I can't Worship the Lord every second of the day, or in every little opportunity that comes my way. I'm not in heaven yet!"

Neither am I. None of us can do all these things every day, any more than we could eat every dish offered on a huge smorgasbord. But it *is* wonderful to have so many dishes from which to choose. It is just with this encouraging offer of the wide variety of ways to Worship God that this book was written.

Even the devout Brother Lawrence realized that some of us Worship the Lord with greater ease than others. He wrote: "Everyone is able to have these familiar conversations with God, some more, some less—he knows our capabilities." Brother Lawrence also admitted that "some perseverance was needed at first to form the habit of conversing at all times with God and referring all actions to him." Like any new habit or discipline, there is a need for persistence—but not guilt.

The Lord does not want us to feel guilty anytime we are not Worshiping Him. He has put us in this world, which is filled with many responsibilities and necessities. In Mark's gospel, Jesus Himself condemned His contemporaries who ignored family duties supposedly in order to be more devoted to God (see Mark 7:10–12).

It is not a question of Worshiping God and ignoring everyone else, including those in your care. It is a question of priorities. We are called to put God first—that is, to put our relationship with Him before all others. But to use the term *first* presupposes that there be a second, third, fourth or fifth. The supremacy of our bond with Christ does not mean that we neglect the others in our lives.

For most of us, Worshiping God more does not necessitate spending less time with our families or our responsibilities. But it may indeed mean spending less time vegetating, or watching television, or other activities of lesser importance. Our motivation for this should not be guilt but a desire to know the Lord more deeply.

Each of us must prayerfully examine our own lives to find the critical balance of how we can best spend our time and thoughts for God's glory. Even the smallest efforts have value. Goethe urged those around him to "always hold fast to the present hour. Every state of duration, every second, is of infinite value."

A Sure Block to Building Relationship

While we have sampled many dishes from that "smorgasbord" of ways to Worship God, we need to be aware that all of our efforts will be for naught if we fail in one important area. A number of Scriptures indicate that our prayers to God—no matter how fervent—are ineffectual and unacceptable if we allow ongoing sin in our lives. For example:

If I had cherished sin in my heart, the Lord would not have listened.

Psalm 66:18

209

> But your iniquities have separated you from your God; your sins
> have hidden his face from you, so that he will not hear.
>
> Isaiah 59:2

The same is true of Worship. If we harbor unconfessed sin,
all of our attempts at Worship will be in vain. We may go through
the motions of Worship, but we will fail to obtain a two-way
relationship with the Lord.

Last week, my wife and I were shopping together in a large
department store. As I had nothing to buy and she had several
items of clothing to try on, I found myself aimlessly pushing a
shopping cart and waiting. I thought, *I should spend some time Worshiping God,* which I did. Yet soon I realized that I was not Worshiping but becoming more and more impatient with my wife.

Again I tried to Worship; my annoyance at the long wait grew.
Worship ceased altogether. My initial (and typical) reaction was
to blame my wife: "It's all *her* fault that I can't seem to Worship
God tonight!" But the Lord convicted me that the real problem
was *within me:* My sin of impatience had become a barrier
between God and myself.

An important requirement for true Worship is purity. A beautiful image of Worship is given in Psalm 24:3, that of "ascending the hill of the Lord." But the very next verse gives the necessary requirements:

> Who may ascend the hill of the LORD? Who may stand in his
> holy place? He who has *clean hands and a pure heart,* who does
> not lift up his soul to an idol or swear by what is false.
>
> Psalm 24:3–4, emphasis added

Clean hands refers to our actions. *A pure heart* refers to our
motives, the unseen reasons behind our actions. *Lifting up one's
soul to an idol* refers to *anything* that can come between God and
us. And *swearing by what is false* refers to the all-important realm
of our speech.

Without purity in these four critical areas of our lives, our Worship will be powerless. When Brother Lawrence wrote a passage entitled "Means of Attaining the Presence of God," the first two sections were as follows:

1. The *first* means is a great purity of life.
2. The *second* is a great faithfulness in the practice of the presence of God.

Yet many battles that are waged in our various areas of temptation become lifetime struggles. As we seek to become more Christlike, we will always face these two challenges.

Thus, first, we should consciously seek to live a more sin-free life. Taking an honest assessment of our inconsistent dispositions, we should note those areas of sin to which we are naturally prone. These must be attentively avoided, and we should make ourselves accountable in these specific spheres of temptation with the help of wise and trusted friends.

Paul constantly admonishes us about avoiding sin, even using the dynamic one-word command: Flee! "Flee from sexual immorality," (1 Corinthians 6:18); "Flee from idolatry," (1 Corinthians 10:14); "Flee the evil desires of youth," (2 Timothy 2:22); "Flee from *all* this," (1 Timothy 6:11, emphasis added).

And, second, we should make time for regular confession to God. As much as we are commended to avoid sin, we are also forewarned that it will happen. Fortunately, the Lord has designed a remedy for this inevitable cycle. It is called confession, which entails asking the Lord for forgiveness.

Through this incredible and utterly available process, we can be "washed white as snow" and again approach God in true Worship. In the words of King David: "I said, 'I will confess my transgressions to the LORD'—and you forgave the guilt of my sin" (Psalm 32:5). When the people repented at the preaching of John the Baptist, they were baptized after "confessing their sins" (Matthew 3:6). And 1 John 1:9 assures us, "if we confess our sins,

211

he is faithful and just and will forgive us our sins and purify us from all unrighteousness."

Preparing for Heaven

Perhaps the quintessential passage on the subject of Worship is Romans 12:1–2, which is the nucleus of this monumental letter. Before citing these key verses, let's look at what immediately precedes them—as Paul bursts into an ecstatic state of spontaneous Worship:

> Oh, the depth of the riches of the wisdom and knowledge of God! How unsearchable his judgments, and his paths beyond tracing out! "Who has known the mind of the Lord? Or who has been his counselor? Who has ever given to God, that God should repay him?" For from him and through him and to him are all things. To him be the glory forever! Amen.
>
> Romans 11:33–36

It is as if Paul, after such an exultant expression of Worship, now tells us *how* we are to Worship the Lord:

> Therefore, I urge you, brothers, in view of God's mercy, to offer your bodies as living sacrifices, holy and pleasing to God—*this is your spiritual act of worship.* Do not conform any longer to the pattern of this world, but be transformed by the renewing of your mind. Then you will be able to test and approve what God's will is—his good, pleasing and perfect will.
>
> Romans 12:1–2

Many Christians who are familiar only with *corporate* worship are puzzled by this Scripture. They see the words *this is your spiritual act of worship,* but they have inward questions: *Worship? What about singing? What about the church service? What about the choir? What does this passage have to do with worship?*

212

Now that we are familiar with private Worship as a lifestyle we can immediately perceive the lessons Paul is teaching:

1. *Offer your bodies as living sacrifices:* Our entire lives (that is, our lifestyles) are to be spent Worshiping the Lord.
2. *Do not conform any longer to the pattern of this world:* Do not waste our time vegetating as the world does.
3. *Be transformed by the renewing of your mind:* Use our minds to Worship God whenever possible.
4. *Test and approve what God's will is:* Worshiping brings us into relationship so as to find God's divine guidance for our lives.

Now we see that Paul was indeed referring to true Worship. He was training us for an eternity of Worshiping. For indeed, our best training for heaven is Worship. It brings heaven down to us, and *into* us. The Christian teacher Henry Ward Beecher once remarked, "Heaven will be the endless portion of every man who has heaven in his soul."

Different Christian teachers may offer us various explanations of what heaven will be like for us, but all agree on one point: It will include a perpetuation of Worshiping God. Augustine taught that "the sole purpose of life in time is to gain merit for life in eternity." The Bible tells us plainly that "all nations will come and worship before [Him]" (Revelation 15:4).

The Goal: A Life of Worship

Let us end with a few elemental questions: Why are we here? Why were we created? What are our most important duties? And finally, How should we best spend the time we have on this earth?

Each of us must answer these inquiries, if only by default. That is, even if we never formally address such lofty issues as the first three questions, they are ultimately answered by the fourth. For it is in *the way we spend our time* that we announce to all—to

God, to the world and to ourselves—how we would answer the most important questions of our lives.

Comparing the different ways we often spend our time, Brother Lawrence taught: "We should fix ourselves firmly in the presence of God by conversing all the time with him. A shameful course it would be to abandon his fellowship to give thought to trifles."

If we spend time on work, hobbies and other projects yet seldom with the Lord, what does this say about our value of God?

If we spend time thinking about our plans, problems and dozens of trivialities yet seldom ponder the ways of God, what does this say about our love of God?

If we spend time with endless entertainment, becoming spectators of life instead of participants in His work, what does this say about our willingness to be used by God for His purposes?

And if we only worship God in specific settings—in groups on Sunday while being led by others—what does that say about our *personal relationship* with the Lord?

A true relationship does not limit expression merely to certain times and preplanned places. Suppose I kissed my wife only once each week in a specific place in our house. If you observed such an odd ritual, you would surely conclude that the relationship between my wife and me must be rather formal and cold.

Of course I kiss my wife when she wakes up, and when she walks down the hall, and when she is working in the kitchen, and when she sits at the table. There is no "standard time and place" for a husband to kiss his wife. If they truly love each other, then he delights in giving her a kiss and she delights in receiving it.

So it is—even more so!—in our relationship with the Lord. For our last thought on Worship is that God Himself has an overwhelming desire to meet together with you, whenever and wherever possible. He longs to have ongoing communion together, not only on certain days at specific times. The God who created all the wonders of our universe wants one thing of you more than anything else: your heart.

As Brother Lawrence lay quietly on his deathbed, he was asked what he was doing and what accompanied his thoughts. He gently replied, "I am doing what I shall do through all eternity. I am blessing God, praising him, worshiping him, and loving him with all of my heart."

The shepherd boy David, who was made king over all his land and could have almost anything his heart desired, stated: "One thing I ask of the LORD, this is what I seek: that I may dwell in the house of the LORD all the days of my life, to gaze upon the beauty of the LORD and to seek him in his temple" (Psalm 27:4).

Stop reading now, put the book down and Worship your Lord. Worship Him often, today and all days.

Index

Dr. Patrick Kavanaugh is the author of seven books: *Worship—A Way of Life* (Chosen), *The Spiritual Lives of the Great Composers* (Zondervan), *Raising Musical Kids* (Vine), *Music of the Great Composers* (Zondervan), *Spiritual Moments with the Great Composers* (Zondervan), *The Music of Angels: A Listener's Guide to Sacred Music, from Chant to Christian Rock* (Loyola) and *Devotions from the World of Music* (Cook). As a composer he currently has eighteen compositions published by Carl Fischer, Inc. and licensed by Broadcast Music, Inc. (BMI). Patrick has composed in a wide variety of genre, from orchestral to chamber music, from opera to electronic music. Reviews or articles concerning his original works and premieres have appeared in many national magazines, including *Music Journal, Christianity Today* and *Charisma*, and in major newspapers such as *The Washington Post, The New York Times* and *The Washington Times*.

He has served as director of the Washington branch of the National Association of Composers, as the classical music reviewer for *Audio* magazine in New York City and as minister of music at the Christian Assembly Center and the King's Chapel. For three years he was appointed to music panels of the National Endowment for the Arts. Patrick has lectured extensively at many universities and churches and at the National Portrait Gallery and the U.S. Department of State, and he has appeared on many music and talk shows of both radio and TV.

Dr. Kavanaugh's education includes a doctor of musical arts and a master of music from the University of Maryland, where he was awarded a full graduate fellowship for three years, and a bachelor of music from the CUA School of Music. He has also done extensive post-doctoral work in musicology, music theory and conducting. His teachers have included Earle Brown, Conrad Bernier, Mark Wilson and Lloyd Geisler. At the university level he has taught composition, music theory, music history and literature, counterpoint, orchestration and electronic music.

In addition to conducting many premieres of his own works, Kavanaugh was the conductor of the UM Twentieth Century Ensemble and the CUA Summer Orchestra. He now conducts regularly with the Asaph Ensemble. He also appears regularly as a conductor at the Kennedy Center Concert Hall and Terrace Theatre, Constitution Hall, the Center for the Arts, the Lisner Auditorium, the Alden Theatre, the National Presbyterian Center, Tawes Auditorium, the Folger Theatre and Gaston Hall. In 1993 he became the first American conductor invited to conduct an opera at Moscow's Bolshoi Theatre.

Patrick now serves full time as executive director of the Christian Performing Artists' Fellowship, representing more than one thousand members from fifty different denominations. He is also the artistic director of the MasterWorks Festival in New York State. He resides near Washington, D.C., with his wife, Barbara, a cellist, and their four children.

To contact Dr. Kavanaugh:

The Christian Performing Artists' Fellowship
P.O. Box 800
Haymarket, VA 20168
Phone: (703) 753-0334
Fax: (703) 753-0336
e-mail: CPAF@erols.com

The Christian Performing Artists' Fellowship

The Christian Performing Artists' Fellowship (CPAF) is a non-denominational ministry dedicated to performing to the glory of God and to spreading the Gospel in the world of the performing arts. Begun in Washington, D.C., in 1984, it has grown to include more than one thousand members from more than fifty different denominations. It has presented Christ-centered performances from Washington's Kennedy Center to Moscow's Bolshoi Theatre, from Dallas' Meyerson Hall to Bethlehem Square in Israel. *Christianity Today* notes that CPAF "strives to bring the Gospel to a relatively overlooked group: the secular arts world." The *National Christian Reporter* calls CPAF members "missionaries" who are "all dedicated to bring the Gospel of Christ to those who might otherwise not hear it." The Christian Performing Artists' Fellowship is a registered non-profit, tax-exempt organization. All expenses are met by donations. For more information about CPAF call 888–836-CPAF (2723) toll-free.

The MasterWorks Festival

The MasterWorks Festival is a world-class performing arts festival for young performers who want to use their talents for the glory of God. Its faculty includes some of the greatest Christian performers and teachers in the music world. For one month, dozens of high school and college-aged students come together

223

for programs in orchestra, chamber music, piano, opera, theater and dance. The mission of the MasterWorks Festival is to train Christian performing artists in two distinct areas: (1) excellence in their performance skills, and (2) excellence in their Christian walk and witness. The atmosphere of the festival is a combination of serious music-making and studying with the joy of a dedicated Christian environment. Although the time is filled with rehearsals, performances, private lessons and masterclasses, there is also time for devotionals, Bible studies, prayer meetings, worship and fellowship. For more information about or applications for the MasterWorks Festival, see the web site at <www.ChristianPerformingArt.org>.

The MasterClass Bible Studies for Musicians

A unique Bible study guide for musicians has been designed by Patrick Kavanaugh and John Langlois. The "MasterClass Bible Studies" covers a great number of scriptural topics related to the performing arts. The material applies biblical principles to such issues as practicing, performing, relationships, nervousness, teaching, competition and musical careers. These Bible studies are generally used in small groups, many of which meet in professional ensembles as well as music schools. The studies are designed to encourage maximum participation and fellowship in each group. As a service to Christian musicians, CPAF provides copies of the MasterClass Bible Studies free of charge. They can be printed from CPAF's website <www.ChristianPerformingArt.org>.